BUT HOW WILL YOU RAISE THE CHILDREN?

What Do You Do . . .

When you have fallen seriously in love with a person of another faith—and your parents don't want you to marry?
  (see Chapters 1 and 5)

If your parents refuse to attend your wedding?
  (see Chapter 6)

When you've converted to your spouse's religion—but you still miss the holiday traditions of your youth?
  (see Chapter 10)

When you and your spouse disagree about your children's religious education?
  (see Chapters 11 through 13)

If your parents try to influence your children's beliefs?
  (see Chapter 13)

Most Pocket Books are available at special quantity discounts for bulk purchases for sales promotions, premiums or fund raising. Special books or book excerpts can also be created to fit specific needs.

For details write the office of the Vice President of Special Markets, Pocket Books, 1230 Avenue of the Americas, New York, New York 10020.

A GUIDE TO INTERFAITH MARRIAGE

BUT HOW WILL YOU RAISE THE CHILDREN?

Steven Carr Reuben

3443

PUBLISHED BY POCKET BOOKS NEW YORK

This book is dedicated to the woman who fills my life with laughter, song, and love. She has always believed in me, given me strength, filled my heart with courage, inspired me to reach for the best that lies within, and blessed my life with a love to rival any fairy tale. To my partner, my soul mate, my wife—my Didi . . . and to my little girl Gable, whose smile lights up her "abba's" life.

An *Original* publication of POCKET BOOKS

 POCKET BOOKS, a division of Simon & Schuster, Inc., 1230 Avenue of the Americas, New York, N.Y. 10020

ISBN: 0-671-64369-X

First Pocket Books trade paperback printing December, 1987

10 9 8 7 6 5 4 3 2 1

POCKET and colophon are trademarks of Simon & Schuster, Inc.

Printed in the U.S.A.

Foreword

In a recent play, one of the characters, a publisher, remarks to a colleague: "And religion is coming back. You can tell because people are again killing each other in its name." It is true, of course, that religion always has and always will continue to evoke not only deep convictions and strong emotions, but fanaticism and cruelty. That in itself provides no ground for rejecting religion as such. After all, by its very nature, it raises and tries to answer the most fundamental questions of human existence, questions for which people will always seek answers.

A basic premise of this book is that marriages likely to succeed are marriages in which couples share a common religious background and faith. But Rabbi Reuben is a realist. He fully recognizes that the world in which we live is a pluralistic one, possessed of an endless variety of visions and commitments, from the ecstatic to the rigorously logical. That is the world in which people meet and fall in love and decide to marry. And that is the world into which their children will be born.

Each spouse carries along the religious and/or secular convictions instilled during childhood and growing-up. Those convictions can be a treasured gift or a heavy burden, but whichever they are, they will be brought to the marriage feast as part of the gifts to be shared. One may not always agree with Rabbi Reuben's suggestions for incorporating them into the new reality taking shape as a consequence of the couple's decision, but he is commendably provocative and addresses all the issues. His approach is pragmatic; what works for one marriage may not work for another. And it is his own rich pastoral experience which provides him with the necessary casuistry for dealing comprehensively and tolerantly with interfaith marriages.

Is there a more challenging task set before all of us in today's world than that of nurturing and sustaining family life for tomorrow's? This book makes a genuine contribution to that supremely important enterprise.

—REVEREND JOSEPH W. GOETZ

CONTENTS

Introduction   9

Part One
THE INTERFAITH RELATIONSHIP   13

   I. The Dating Game   15
  II. Meeting Your Partner's Family   24
 III. Discussing Religion Together   33
 IV. Should We Get Married?   55

Part Two
THE INTERFAITH WEDDING   73

   V. How to Tell Your Parents "We're Getting
      Married!"   75
  VI. Planning the Wedding   96
 VII. Conversion   117
VIII. Tying the Knot   126

Part Three
THE INTERFAITH MARRIAGE   135

  IX. Living with Differences   137
   X. Creating Your Own Religious Life-Style   159

Part Four
CHILDREN OF THE INTERFAITH MARRIAGE   183

   XI. "But How Will You Raise the Children?"   185
  XII. In Their Own Words—What Children Say   200
XIII. Grandparents—Obstacles or Opportunities   211

Part Five
WHEN THINGS DON'T WORK OUT   223

  XIV. Breaking Up an Interfaith Relationship   225

Part Six
EXPERIENCE CAN BE THE BEST TEACHER   239

  XV. Advice from Those Who Have Been There   241

Interfaith marriage is one of the great spiritual challenges of our time; Catholics are marrying Protestants, Methodists are marrying Lutherans, Baptists are marrying Episcopalians. There are currently 300,000 to 400,000 Jewish/non-Jewish interfaith marriages alone in America, and the numbers increase annually.

The very face of religion in America is being steadily transformed. We no longer live in a neat patchwork quilt of distinct faiths and communities, with clear, well-differentiated ideological boundaries.

For over fifteen years, as I have worked in my role as rabbi with hundreds of interfaith couples and their extended families, I have seen the pain, confusion, turmoil, indecision, and insecurity that so often accompany a decision to marry someone of another religious background. I have constantly been called upon to give advice and counsel to the couples, their parents, in-laws, and children, as they painfully worked their ways through the many decisions, problems, and choices that are an inevitable part of interfaith life.

As a rabbi, my primary life work is dedicated to enhancing the quality and vitality of Jewish life in America. I also believe that people have the best chance for marital success if their relationship is built on a strong foundation of shared values, life experiences, and culture. For these reasons and others, I strongly believe that same-faith marriages are preferable, and neither I nor any of the national rabbinic associations in North America encourage interfaith marriages.

At the same time I recognize that with or without our approval, such marriages will continue in ever increasing numbers. I therefore continue to reach out to such couples, both privately and through this book, so that those who choose an interfaith relationship will in spite of the odds have the best possible chance of success.

Often the families have asked if I could recommend a good counseling book that addressed these important issues that are such an everyday part of the lives of interfaith families. Realizing that nothing existed that quite fit the bill, I decided to write this book. It is a way for me to share not only my own years of experience in counseling interfaith families, but the real-life experiences of actual (though anonymous) interfaith couples, parents, and children who have graciously shared their stories with me.

The impact of divorce, remarriage, and the often resultant blended interfaith family has had a profound impact on the reality of religious life as well. As family life continues to undergo the steady transformation from "Father knows best" to "Which father am I living with today?" the effects on traditional religious affiliations and identifications are dramatic. No longer is American society neatly divided into Protestant/Catholic/Jewish. Today you may very likely discover *all three* and more living together under one extended-family roof.

The challenge for the individual couple remains—how to create a loving, supporting, nourishing, and sustained relationship in the face of tremendous forces that constantly work to tear them apart.

This book is written both for those who have already married and for those who are still thinking and deciding. It is here to serve as a private guide and counselor to those caught up in the tugs and pulls of an interfaith relationship, without pressure from parents, friends, siblings, husbands, wives, or children. It is an opportunity to spend time alone thinking about how best to cope with the everyday stresses and issues of interfaith marriage. It is designed for you alone, to give you the chance to use the experiences of other couples in other circumstances to apply to your own life.

Together we shall listen to the voices of men and women of all ages and religious backgrounds as they share their stories with us and invite us into their lives. We will learn firsthand how they have successfully dealt with the same problems that you will be or have already been facing. I hope their anecdotes, coupled with my own years of experience counseling interfaith couples, will help you to make decisions that will add a greater sense of control, joy, and satisfaction to your relationship and to your life.

We will look at the typical problems that interfaith relationships must face, in the order in which they usually occur. Beginning with dating, we will cover discussing religion together, clarifying religious values and beliefs, dealing with parents and potential in-laws, choosing whether or not to get married, deciding on the ceremony itself, converting or not, creating your own religious life-style, and raising children.

I believe that in spite of numerous potential stumbling blocks, interfaith marriages are filled with opportunities for growth and self-satisfaction. All relationships take tremendous commitment, which is especially true for interfaith relationships. Such relationships need even more nurturing, tolerance, and willingness to do whatever is in your power to see the world through another's eyes and to struggle to understand their perspective, dreams, and needs.

Interfaith marriages *can* be filled with the excitement of a successful loving partnership, and the constant thrills of precious moments of encountering the depth and soul of another human being. I have dedicated this book to helping interfaith couples make that dream a reality.

_____ *Part One*

THE
INTERFAITH
RELATIONSHIP

Chapter I

THE DATING GAME

"I believe that deep-rooted warnings from very early training and upbringing go off in every interfaith relationship."

—Monica, therapist in an interfaith marriage

It was a college romance. Jim and Susan* met in biology class in their freshman year at a typical Ivy League college.

They began exchanging class notes, then walking to class together, eating lunch on the lawn, and filling their hours discussing school, politics, and the future of our troubled world in this nuclear age.

Their relationship soon turned to romance, carrying with it the flush of new-love excitement, and the thrill that comes from discovering another human being who shares your dreams and has a similar outlook on the world.

By the time of their graduation, they were thoroughly in love and planned their wedding for the end of the summer. They both assumed that their families would not only expect the marriage, but would be excited and happy for them, since they had spent alternate vacations visiting one set of parents or the other for several years.

The day that Jim and Susan formally announced their wedding plans to their parents, Susan received the shock of her life. Her

---

*Jim and Susan are real people, as are all the couples in this book. Names have been changed throughout to protect their privacy.

parents, who had always seemed to like Jim very much and warmly welcomed him into their home for holidays and vacations, angrily announced that although Jim was "a very nice young man," they were one hundred percent against Susan's marrying him. Moreover, they were upset, disappointed, and hurt that she could seriously consider it.

Jim fared only slightly better with his parents. They too were unhappy about his choice of Susan as a wife (although "she is a lovely girl and we have always been quite fond of her"), and they hoped that Jim understood the possible implications of what he was doing.

Jim and Susan were both dumbfounded. They just couldn't understand why their parents seemed to accept without judgment or criticism the years of dating, yet angrily rejected the mere mention of marriage as if it were some kind of personal betrayal.

Jim was Christian and Susan was Jewish. They had never encountered prejudice regarding their relationship before, and had found each other so intellectually and morally compatible, that it simply never occurred to them that religion would ever be a problem. Suddenly, they were thrust into a confrontation with their differences and the fears of their parents, and both were totally unprepared for the encounter.

Neither of them could understand why their parents objected to their marriage so strenuously. "After all," Susan said, "of course I was raised to know that I was Jewish, but my family was never particularly religious. I don't understand why all of a sudden my parents feel so strongly about Judaism when they never went to temple—except perhaps once a year on the High Holidays—and didn't even care whether I went to a Jewish religious school or not."

Jim, on the other hand, was distressed at what he perceived to be possible anti-Semitic prejudice among his family. Since he hadn't gone to church since he was twelve years old, he couldn't understand his parents' objections either.

Susan's parents kept asking her where they had gone wrong, why she was rejecting Judaism, and how could she ever raise Christian children after all that the Jews had been through over the centuries.

Jim's parents kept reminding him that although *they* had no prejudices, there were still those in the rest of the community who did, and asked how would he feel about raising children who didn't believe in Jesus.

Jim and Susan both knew that they loved each other, and were certain that their love would be strong enough to overcome any obstacles. "We have a lot more in common than we have differences," Jim would say, "and I'm sure that we can work everything out if we keep communicating with one another as well as we always have."

"I agree," Susan added. "The most important thing is for us to share our feelings with each other and talk to one another. We have always worked things out in the past and I'm sure that we can do it now. Anyway, neither of us is particularly religious and it hasn't really been much of an influence in our lives. In fact, it really never came up in our relationship at all.

"I love the chance to celebrate Christmas with Jim and his family since I never got to celebrate it as a kid. Ever since we've been going together, I've invited Jim to come to my parents' house for the Passover Seder, too."

By the time Jim and Susan walked into my office, they had already set the wedding date. They had talked it over and discovered that Jim didn't particularly care who married them. Susan said that although she couldn't really explain why, she would feel a lot better if they were married by a rabbi.

Someone who had been at an interfaith wedding that I had performed gave them my name, and so like hundreds of couples before them, they sat feeling slightly nervous across the desk from me. With all the exuberance and idealism of their youth, they were convinced that their love for one another would allow them to overcome every potential problem that might arise.

This book is for Jim and Susan, and the thousands of interfaith couples like them, who face similar challenges in their relationships. Nearly all interfaith couples struggle with the same issues, confront the same obstacles, and find themselves searching for answers to the same questions.

If they are fortunate, they create the opportunity to discuss these issues early on in their relationships, before the problems themselves arise. If not, they often find themselves long into a marriage, with children on the way, before discovering that they have serious conflicts that they are unprepared for emotionally, psychologically, and spiritually.

Jim and Susan had a good foundation upon which to build understanding and trust, two of the crucial keys to a successful interfaith relationship.

The first thing we did together was to try to identify stereotypes, which are a normal but usually unacknowledged part of every interfaith relationship, by using word associations.

For example, when I said "cross," Jim said "Jesus" and Susan said "killing." When I said "Jew," Susan responded "religion" and Jim answered "family." I said "Christmas," Jim replied "presents," and Susan said "exciting."

Through this simple exercise, they discovered that in fact religion and religious thinking were very much a part of their respective backgrounds. They realized that they had both adopted many preconceived ideas and beliefs from their parents, schools, the mass media, and peers. Some of these ideas and associations were potential time bombs in their relationship, which, if not exposed and dealt with openly and honestly, might simply blow up in their faces later.

Susan told me, "I never realized that I had any feelings whatsoever about religion. It just didn't occur to me since it didn't seem to be an important part of my life. I never really thought much about it until now, but I see how I have unconsciously picked up lots of ideas and expectations about Jews, Christians, and all the other things that you stirred up.

"I guess I do have a lot of feelings associated with religious symbols like the cross, Star of David, Jesus, and even Christians as a whole. It kind of makes me mad, as if I had been subtly brainwashed as a child and I didn't even know it."

I assured both of them that "brainwashing" was a bit strong to describe the normal process of religious acculturation in our society, and that some significant influences from their respective religions was inevitable.

"We never really had to make a conscious choice about interfaith dating," Jim mused. "It was just that we liked each other and started spending more and more time together. In college, religion isn't much of an issue for most kids. It's more like something that you do at home with your parents, and at school all you care about is passing classes and having a good time. I still think that for Susan and me religion won't be a problem. It's only our parents who seem to be making more than it is out of it."

Studies of interfaith marriage show that half of all interfaith couples meet either at college or at work. This has prompted some who are concerned about the high rate of interfaith marriage to suggest, tongue in cheek, that the best way to reduce interfaith marriage is simply to discourage young people from going to college.

By the time a young man or woman does go to college, it is unlikely that exhortations or warnings from worried parents will have much impact on their dating habits. As Susan explained, "I certainly wouldn't have asked Jim, 'Excuse me, but what religion are you?' before I went out with him. Even if it had mattered to me, which it didn't, I'd be much too embarrassed to ask a question like that.

"You just go out with whomever you are attracted to. Besides, when you start dating someone, you aren't thinking about marrying them, you are just concerned with whether or not you like them enough to go out. I don't know anyone who examines every potential date as a serious marriage partner. If you did that you'd probably never go out with anyone."

Susan is a perfect example of how most young people feel. The thought of checking the religious pedigree and background of every potential date is enough to make any red-blooded college student laugh. Of course, it is exactly because of this contemporary reality that we have seen the dramatic rise in interfaith marriages over the past few decades.

Interfaith dating is the cause of interfaith marriage. Yet, few young people are willing to limit their dating experiences and choices to those of the same religion. There are those, however, who do give the issue serious thought and concern. Often I have seen young people in the throes of self-criticism and doubt, worried because they are increasingly involved with someone of another religious background, and worried as to the long-term implications of their actions.

Such a young man was Scott. He called my office one day

during winter break and asked if he might spend a few minutes with me. He said only, "I have some questions about marriage and religion that I'd like to ask you."

When he came into my study, I could see immediately that he was filled with inner turmoil. In response to my gentle prodding, he shared with me the nature of his conflict.

"I am in my second year of college," he began, "and have been dating a girl named Mindy fairly regularly for the past year. At first I was attracted to her because she seemed so different from the girls I had known in high school. And of course she is great looking, which didn't hurt.

"Anyway, we get along great and spend as much time together as we can. I certainly love her more than I have ever loved anyone, but in the past couple of months the relationship has begun to scare me.

"Every time I am with her family, which has only been a few times during vacations, I have felt uncomfortable. At first I thought it was just that I didn't know them, and that I was nervous because I wanted to make a good impression and have them like me. But after the third time I was with them, I realized that it was the difference in our background and upbringing that kept bothering me.

"It's almost as if, when we are alone, just the two of us at school, there isn't any difference between us at all. But as soon as we are with her family or mine, the differences suddenly are staring me in the face. It is really upsetting me because I never thought I would find myself in this situation, and I don't know what to do about it.

"I could use some advice. Since I know that you spend a lot of time with interfaith couples, I thought that perhaps you might have some insights into my situation. What do you think I should do? Do you think I should stop seeing Mindy? Am I blowing the whole thing out of proportion, so that something that isn't really a problem at all seems like a problem? Help!"

What could I say to Scott that he didn't already know? He already knew that he was growing closer and closer to Mindy, and that whenever he faced the reality of their different upbringings honestly, he became agitated and ill at ease. He already knew that it was *because* religion was an important part of his identity that he was upset in the first place, and he already knew that he had a limited number of options.

I pointed out that it seemed he had only three choices. First, he could ignore the religious differences and let whatever happened happen. Second, he could separate himself from the anxiety by ending the relationship with Mindy and making sure that the next time he got involved with a girl, she would be of his own religion. Third, he could confront Mindy with his feelings, share his anxieties and understanding of their source with her, and see if there was a way that together they could solve the problem.

Scott thought it over for a moment. "I think that really the only way that I will be happy is if she ends up converting to my religion. Otherwise, I am always going to feel that I have cheated myself out of something that is important to me. God, I wish I didn't feel this way. Sometimes I hate what religion does to separate people from each other."

Scott was suffering because he was mature enough to realize that, in a sense, all dating is potential courtship and carries within it the seeds of a potential marriage. Every time a young man and woman begin a relationship, they are testing the waters of commitment and possibly starting down the road to inner conflict and religious turmoil.

I could empathize with his suffering since I recalled a time in my own youth when I broke off a relationship with someone I cared for, simply because she was of a different religious background, and I knew that ultimately it just wouldn't work.

Even the conflicts that may arise out of interfaith dating can be a positive force for crystallizing a more solid sense of self for the individuals involved. I pointed out to Scott that in a sense interfaith dating can be a form of religious values clarification. It is an opportunity for an individual to discover how important religion and family background really are in his or her life. In a sense, it was because of his relationship with Mindy that Scott had the opportunity to experience clearly for himself the place religion had in his life.

Most young people simply have no idea of the role, significant or not, that religion plays in their self-definition. They don't know in advance whether it will make any difference if their boyfriend or girlfriend shares their religious background. Only after they have experienced the differences, after they have been exposed to another set of parents, another life-style, another set of religious values and celebrations, will they know how they feel about the importance of their own religion.

Yet, interfaith dating alone obviously does not guarantee that a couple will be able to clarify the relative importance of religion in their lives. Instead, most of the couples that I have worked with and spoken to on the subject of interfaith marriage suffer from what I call the Romeo and Juliet syndrome.

Just as Romeo and Juliet were carried away to irrational and totally romantic behavior by their love, so too most interfaith couples sit in my office with stars in their eyes and say, "Love conquers all." They fervently believe that simply loving each other is enough to cause every serious problem or conflict to vanish like the early morning fog in the face of a rising sun.

Love *is* a wonderful thing. In fact, as far as I am concerned it is *the* most wonderful thing on earth. It is a gift of the spirit that lets us know we all have the capacity for expressing a spark of divinity through a loving relationship with another human being.

Yet love does not conquer all. It does not erase the feelings of dis-ease when a believing Baptist brings his girlfriend to church, only to hear her ask, "How can you believe all that stuff about heaven and hell?"

It does not eliminate a Jewish girl's feelings of anxiety at the impending holiday visit of her parents to the home she shares with a non-Jewish boyfriend, when she knows they will see the Christmas tree in *her* home for the first time.

It does not stifle the quiet, nagging self-doubt that new Catholic parents feel when they don't baptize their child out of "respect" for the Jewish side of the family.

Love is the best foundation that any couple could have for building a lasting, mutually supportive, and satisfying relationship. But as forty-two-year-old Walter, who has been involved in an interfaith marriage for fifteen years, told me, "There are some things in life that you just can't love away."

In every interfaith relationship there are moments of tension, issues that must be resolved, problems to be overcome.

Chapter II will plunge us immediately into one of the most sensitive experiences of an interfaith relationship—meeting your partner's family. You might want to read it over not only before your first encounter with them, but prior to any visit, as long as tensions or problems continue to exist in the relationship.

MEETING YOUR
PARTNER'S FAMILY

"The beginning with our families was the
most difficult time."

—John, forty-one, interfaith married sixteen years

Clearly one of the most anxious moments in the life of an interfaith couple is the first encounter with the partner's parents. No
matter how old we become, how "important" we are in our work
and profession, how long we have been involved with the person
we love, and how many relationships we have had in our lives, on
some level we all still want our parents' approval.

Each of us wants our parents to somehow let us know that they
think we have done well for ourselves, that we are a success in
their eyes. This desire is just one of the reasons why the first
meeting of the one you love with your parents is fraught with
anxiety.

Most of the time you are actually more worried about how your
parents will accept your partner than about how your partner's
parents will accept you. After all, you know that your partner
loves you, and for you that is probably enough. While it would be
nice if his/her parents think you are the best match since Bogie
and Bacall, if it doesn't happen, it isn't the end of the world.

How *your* parents react, however, is an entirely different story.
To a child, and all of us have some child in us, acknowledged or
not, parental approval is a sign of parental love. When they reject

something you like, it is experienced as a rejection of *you* as much as it is the true object of their disfavor.

Part of the trick to successful first meetings with parents is in recognizing that this psychological mechanism is at work. In doing so, you automatically reduce the potential power your parents hold over the child in you. Nothing scares away the psychological demons of childhood faster than the light of consciousness.

It is also important to discuss your feelings with your partner. Reassure him/her that *your* feelings for him/her have nothing whatsoever to do with the acceptance or rejection of your parents. Let your partner know that your relationship with him/her is totally independent of your relationship with your parents. Although it would certainly be better for everyone if the individual and the relationship received your parents' approval, it isn't a necessary component of the relationship itself.

It's important to reassure each other of the nature of your relationship at high stress moments such as this. The more you see yourselves as partners in each experience and encounter with others from the very beginning of your relationship, the stronger it will be. In Chapter IX we will discuss at some length the concept of a "team marriage." For now, suffice it to say that the more you relate to the rest of the world, including your parents, as a team, the more satisfying and joy-filled will be your relationship.

The first meeting is a kind of elaborate dance where all the participants do their best to smoothly glide from one song to another without their feet ever missing a beat. Undoubtedly, your partner's parents have their own share of concerns, questions, doubts, and anxieties. They most likely would like to react favorably to you and must sort out their own mixed feelings as you all gingerly feel your way through this new experience.

Your partner's parents are in the position of knowing, or at least hoping, that their opinion makes a difference to your partner. This puts a lot of pressure on them to give you a passing grade since, in general, parents don't like to cause their children pain and disappointment.

Rarely do parents reject you or your partner out of hand. If that is their attitude, you usually know all about it in advance. Parents who feel that strongly, and we will meet a number of them throughout this book, are usually very up front about their feelings. They aren't subtle, diplomatic, or tactful in their conversations with you or your partner. They are the ones who call on the phone and, when your partner answers, never acknowledge that they even know who it is. Toward them it's simply, "May I speak to _____, please," period!

Most of the time your first meeting will be pleasant, noncommittal, and if you are smart, brief. The best solution to meeting-the-parents anxiety is to meet them in a setting where something else is going on. Try not to make "the meeting" the focus of everyone's attention, as if it were a state visit to the White House and a Director of Protocol were needed.

The most relaxed meetings take place in informal settings, often almost casually when you are on your way somewhere else. Perhaps you can arrange to go to a show, concert, or special event of some kind and drop in to meet them for a few minutes on your way. This will eliminate an entire evening's being devoted to the encounter itself and will make it more comfortable for everyone.

Meet your partner's parents as early in the relationship as possible. That way the relationship itself is still casual, and there is no "Possible Marriage Partner" sign flashing on your forehead. Many couples have told me how they introduced their partner to their parents within the first month or two, so that whatever happened in the relationship their parents would know whom they were talking about.

In any case, don't expect magnums of champagne, caviar, and balloons with your name printed on them for your first visit. Look at it as simply an opportunity to meet them. Nothing else needs to be accomplished. You don't have to tell them your life story or find out theirs. Yes, it is nice to reveal something about yourself that lets them know you trust them and are an open and communicative person. But don't feel that you must impress her parents with a competent analysis of current stock market trends or share with them the trauma you suffered at age three when your favorite dog died.

Relax. That's my best advice. Be yourself, whatever that may be, and know that ultimately it is only *one* encounter out of the many that will eventually compose their total picture of who you are and the qualities you possess.

"I'll never forget the first time I met Laura's parents," Bill moaned. "I was so uptight about it that first I put a glass of wine down on her polished oak table without a coaster, then realizing what I had done I grabbed for the glass and in the process spilled the entire glass of wine all over everything. I can't ever remember being more embarrassed in my life."

Perhaps he would have felt better at the time if I could have told him that in Judaism wine is a symbol of joy. Then he could have viewed his little mishap as symbolically spreading "joy" all over the living room! Of course, in his case, a more prudent choice would probably have been to partake in a glass or two of "joy" *before* he arrived at her parents' home!

Another idea for reducing the stress of a first meeting is to arrange to meet the parents as part of a larger group. Make sure that there are a few other people around, friends of yours, people you are going out with together. That is the way twenty-four-year-old Shelley handled the problem of introducing her parents to her new boyfriend, Kirk.

"I just invited a bunch of friends to come over to my parents' house to swim, and Kirk was just one of them. It made everyone more comfortable, and it was much easier to have an unpressured conversation with my parents with a number of people involved."

"I felt a lot better," added Kirk. "I could meet Shelley's parents, talk about nothing with them, and do it in the context of a group discussion so everyone was at ease. Also the nature of the event itself—a swim afternoon—was conducive to a relaxed atmosphere."

Introducing One Another

Often couples tell me that they are very concerned about the introduction. "How am I going to introduce her?" asked twenty-year-old Ben. "I think 'This is my girlfriend, Dana' sounds silly. It's too formal and too childish at the same time."

It is even a greater problem for those couples who are divorced or are older. "I certainly wouldn't call Gene, who's thirty-six years old, my 'boyfriend,'" said Maureen. "It sounds so juvenile, but I don't know what else to call him. We don't seem to have any appropriate terms for someone you love in a mature relationship other than 'boyfriend' and 'girlfriend.' Calling him my 'lover' is too intimate a term, and 'friend' just doesn't capture the relationship at all.

"My mother refers to him as 'Maureen's special friend' when she talks about him to her friends, but I am really at a loss as to how to refer to him with my parents."

My advice to Maureen was, Call him Gene! After all, that is his name. Ninety-nine percent of the time you don't really have to give him a label anyway. When in doubt, go for simplicity. It usually works best.

Another tip for easing the introduction jitters is to watch the way you both dress. Physical appearance has a lot to do with how we react to others. It often determines whether or not we feel comfortable with them, our perceptions of the kind of person they are, and even our judgments as to their character. Take the time to think about your appearance, knowing that whether you like it or not, in the beginning your parents will form judgments of your partner in large part as a result of first impressions. After all, in the beginning there is little else to go on.

How to Talk to Parents

A first meeting is a time of stress, even if you do it in a group, set it up on the run to another event, and pay attention to the clothes you wear. Still, you can control to a large extent what actually happens during a first encounter with your partner's parents by preparing for it.

You might ask what kind of preparations you can make for meeting someone's parents. There are in fact several things you can do. First, find out from your partner some interesting things about his/her parents. Where are they from? What is their background? What type of work do they do? What is their family like? How many children? Where do they go on vacation? Perhaps you have intersecting interests, or someone from your family lives in the city, state, or country they came from.

These simple things can be used as the basis of conversations *initiated by you* during your meeting. No matter how sophisticated we may be, everyone's favorite subject of discussion is himself! Capitalize on this fact by directing questions to them, or leading the discussion to topics of conversation that you already know they are interested in.

First meetings are definitely a time to accentuate areas of commonality and not to stress differences. Especially in an interfaith relationship, the differences are already painfully clear to parents before they even think about meeting you. You can score a real public relations coup if you can leave this first encounter having planted seeds of familiarity in their minds.

It is best for both of you to plan a meeting strategy together. In that way you will always feel the support and strength of your relationship, regardless of what actually happens in the meeting itself. Use this as a practice opportunity for relationship building.

All of your life together is, in a sense, a great experiment. You are constantly testing different ways of relating to each other, different strategies for dealing with problems, concerns, and fears that one or the other of you may be experiencing.

Before the first meeting is a perfect time to begin this process if it hasn't happened already. Sit down with your partner and ask, "What can I do to help you get through the stress of this meeting?" or "What do you think we can come up with together to make sure the meeting will be as low-keyed and stress-free as possible?" Then share as many ideas with each other as you can. Write them down as you think of them so that you can go over them later and pick out the best ones to actually use.

Talking to parents *can* be intimidating, but it doesn't have to be. Think about those attributes that *you* look for in someone and then picture yourself exhibiting those characteristics. Imagine a conversation between you and your partner's parents in your mind. Go over what you will say, picture yourself saying it, hear their reactions and your responses.

Visualizing anxious situations in advance is an excellent technique for reducing anxiety. Picture as clearly as you can in your mind exactly what the situation will look like, what you will be wearing, what they will look like, their facial expressions, and as much detail as you can muster. In visualizing, details make the difference—the more the better.

Since your subconscious mind doesn't know the difference

between the visualization and the real thing, your emotional reaction will be similar to what you visualize, and to the extent that the visualization was accurate, you will have been well prepared for the actual meeting.

Above all, be genuine. Don't be excessively flattering or compliment things that you don't actually like. No one likes a phony, and insincerity can only backfire in the end. On the other hand, everyone likes acknowledgment, and to the extent that it can honestly be given, it will make lots of points for you.

"I was really worried about Joan meeting my mom," Roger confessed. "But after she mentioned how beautiful she thought the needlepoint on the wall was, she was golden. My mother prides herself on her needlepoint and has a number of her better pieces framed and hung. I didn't even think to tell Joan in advance, but it worked out perfectly anyway. My mom thinks she is a doll. Some things turn out to be easier than you imagine."

Yes, some things *are* easier than you think. A simple matter of courtesy can seem like a big thing to your loved one's parents. Being genuine, keeping the conversation on topics of interest to the parents, planning in advance, paying attention to how you are dressed and the impression you wish to make, are all easy things to do and indirectly tell others that you really care about them and their feelings.

Breaking Down Initial Resistance

Someone once said that the only person in the world who really likes change is a wet baby. It just seems to be part of human nature for people to fear things they don't know. This resistance is often a part of first meetings with parents.

The best strategy for breaking down these initial fears and barriers is to do your best to make the unknown known. Self-disclosure is one of the best ways to demonstrate your trust of them, and thus to earn it. Psychologists tell us that one of the most effective ways of breaking down emotional barriers between yourself and another is to allow yourself to be perceived as vulnerable. Vulnerability is interpreted by others as a declaration that you are "safe" to be with. You cease to be a threat in any way, and the psychological barriers that otherwise might have existed melt away.

Allow yourself to be vulnerable. People respect someone who feels secure enough in who they are to be willing to share themselves openly with others. It demonstrates a sense of self-worth and can only help soften any potential sharp edges to the initial meeting itself.

The Supportive Partner

The single most important component for a successful parents' meeting is the knowledge that you are going into it with a totally supportive and caring partner. How you react to one another, how you help each other, how you respect each other's needs and fears, has a much more profound impact on the quality of your relationship than *anything* someone's parents could ever do or say.

Holding each other's hands in stressful moments is one of the most important relationship builders I know. Actions always speak louder than words, and you will find that simply being there for the person you love is more important to them than any poem you could ever write or speech you could deliver.

"I remember how nervous I was about the whole thing," Don recalled. "I noticed that my hands were beginning to sweat, and I started having all sorts of horrible premonitions of one disaster or another befalling me. I figured after I met Cherie's parents, and if they rejected me, she would begin to look at me as less desirable too, and the relationship would take a nosedive.

"Then, all of a sudden, as we were getting close to her parents' house, she reached over, held my hand, and gave it a squeeze. After that, somehow I knew everything would work out fine. I just needed to know that Cherie was there for me, that she understood my anxiety and would do whatever she could to help me through it. I got all of that and more out of a simple hand squeeze."

Your physical touch is an important gift that you can give to the one you love. I like to look at it as a form of psychological acupressure. It is an especially important treasure at times of tension or stress.

"It's funny," Sharon told me. "I feel strange saying this, but sometimes I almost feel as if I'm a living electrical circuit, and just touching Hank provides a kind of grounding for my psyche. The physical contact centers me, makes me feel solid and attached to something substantial, and in a way makes me feel stronger and more powerful as well."

Meeting your partner's parents should be looked upon as an opportunity. Every situation in life has the potential for success or failure, pleasure or disappointment. Most of the time *how* you react to a given set of events or circumstances is more important than the circumstances themselves.

You are in control *if* you learn to master your attitude.

Over two thousand years ago a sage wrote, "Who is strong? He who conquers his emotions." Of course today we would say he or she, but the message is the same.

True mastery over your life, and your relationships, lies in the ability to master your emotional response to the circumstances of your life. When Bill spilled the wine at dinner with Laura's parents, he could have allowed it to fluster him even more so that he simply felt stupid and incompetent as a person. He then could have plunged into an emotional depression guaranteed to insure that the rest of the meeting was a disaster. Or, he could have laughed at himself, making light of how nervous he was and how important it was for him to make a good impression on his girlfriend's parents. With this approach, her parents probably would have found him downright charming, if not irresistible.

The choice is always up to you. I have found that if you focus your energy on taking care of your own emotional needs, you will most often be taking care of your partner as well.

I can't emphasize enough the importance of sharing your feelings, fears, anxieties, and needs with each other. A first meeting with your partner's parents can be a golden opportunity to begin a lifelong habit of approaching all stressful encounters as true partners, equally in need of love and mutual support.

Chapter III

DISCUSSING RELIGION TOGETHER

"The most important thing is for the couple to know themselves and their feelings. Don't be blinded by love so that you avoid that which is important to you. Otherwise, you will make decisions and concessions that are not sincere and it will come back to haunt you in the end."

—Judy, forty-three, interfaith married fifteen years

My first impression of Georgia and Frank was of a couple in the midst of heated debate. In the moment between the time I saw them and they first noticed me, I heard enough to guess that here was yet another couple suffering from that universal problem—failure to communicate.

They continued their argument as they entered my study, practically without missing a beat, and I marveled at the stamina and strength of will they both displayed. After another long moment of listening, I finally broke in. "What was it that you came to talk to me about?"

"Oh, I am sorry," said Georgia. "I just get so mad when he doesn't listen to a word that I say. We have had this argument at least a dozen times already, and we never seem to get anywhere. We just keep going round and round in circles all the time."

"It's really not that big a deal," Frank interjected. "I didn't even want to take up your time with such a minor problem, but Georgia kept insisting that we come and talk to you about it. At least that gave us an excuse to argue about something else for a while— whether or not we were even coming!"

"It's like this," Georgia resumed, ignoring Frank's interruption. "We've been going out together for eight months, and we get along great most of the time. The problem is that every now and then he says something like 'How could you really believe all that stuff about Jesus being the Messiah' and we get into an argument. He doesn't understand that Jesus is important to me, and he makes fun of me like I'm some kind of idiot."

"That's not true," Frank protested. "I don't think *you* are an idiot, I just can't understand how in a world so filled with killing, wars, hunger, poverty, and prejudice, *anyone* could believe that a 'Messiah' had already come. If he had, wouldn't the world already be fixed? I really don't try to insult her, Rabbi, I love her. I just get carried away with it whenever I get wound up on 'Jesus.' "

Frank and Georgia didn't know how to talk to one another about religion without ending up yelling at each other. Their plight is certainly not unique. In fact, from my experience, it is the single most common interfaith problem, both before and after marriage.

Time after time I have watched and listened as couples "talk" to each other—or rather *at* each other—about religion, without even coming close to getting the other person to understand their point of view.

For an interfaith relationship to be successful you must be able to talk openly and honestly about your religious beliefs, feelings, needs, and desires. Too often religion becomes the *last* thing such a couple will attempt to discuss, since they are afraid in advance that it will just create friction or distance between them. This oversensitivity to the subject of religion is one of the most common problems that interfaith relationships face.

The real question is, if you are afraid that discussing something that is an important part of who you are will destroy your relationship, how strong do you really think the relationship is? This is your life you are dealing with and the stakes are serious, and high.

Learning to communicate effectively and supportively about

religion is, I believe, one of the most important skills you can ever learn. Without it, your relationship will be one moment after another of walking on emotional eggshells. With it, you will have the freedom to truly share your self with another, to discover that which is important and central to the makeup of the person you love, and the possibility of building together a strong, nurturing, open, and joyous relationship.

Frank and Georgia are typical of hundreds of couples I have counseled. They speak to each other about things they don't understand, using language that means different things to each of them, thereby pushing each other's emotional buttons and precluding any real meeting of the minds every time they "discuss" religion.

I asked Frank if it would be okay with him for Georgia to believe something that he didn't believe. For example, could he accept that she could believe that Jesus was divine, that he had died for the sins of the world, and that through belief in him an individual could achieve salvation?

At first he repeated his assertion that he couldn't understand how anyone could believe all of that "stuff." I replied that as a non-Christian I could understand and sympathize with his feelings. At the same time, I asked him to take a minute to think about whether or not he could accept the fact that someone he loved, in this case Georgia, could possibly hold a different set of religious beliefs, and that those beliefs might in fact be very important to her.

He told me that it *did* bother him that she believed all these things. Since he didn't believe or understand her religious views himself, he saw them as naive and childish, and he had a hard time respecting naive and childish beliefs.

"I guess that's why I always make fun of it all the time," he said. "I am afraid to just say, 'I think you are naive and childish,' since I don't want to insult Georgia, but somewhere deep inside I really think it's silly. I keep hoping that she will just wake up one day and say, 'You know you are right. How could I ever have believed all those silly stories,' but of course it never happens.

"In a sense, I use the arguments to cover up my own fears about the relationship. I don't have any problems with my love for

Georgia; I know that I love her very much. It's only when I put her into the category of a-naive-person-who-believes-silly-things that I actually do and say things that hurt her and the relationship."

I pointed out that there are billions of people on the earth and most of them have their own set of religious beliefs. I asked if he thought that *everyone* who didn't believe as he did was naive, silly, or stupid, or if he could accept the notion that *nobody* really has the ultimate answers to the age-old questions of life. Could he accept the idea that all of us make up our own answers about the essential purpose of life in a way that satisfies us, and that perhaps the most important thing is not what we believe, but rather how we act and interact with others in the world?

When I put it that way he found it much easier to accept religious differences. The three of us then talked about what each of them thought were the really important things in life. I asked them to share with each other what their real values were, how they felt about the world around them, their responsibilities to others, to themselves, to each other. They began to speak about the here and now, rather than life after death and the ultimate reward or punishment that might be waiting down the road, and they realized that despite their differences of theology they did have the same basic attitudes about life.

With Frank and Georgia, as soon as they were able to get past the surface images, "someone who believes in Jesus," "someone who doesn't believe in Jesus," they could talk *to* and not *at* each other. This isn't to say that theological beliefs are not important issues. They are. But here the point I am making is that most of the time, theology is *not* the real issue. Most of the time there are unacknowledged fears and stereotypes, often going back to child-hood, that are the true source of conflict.

In an interfaith relationship you must be able to separate your partner from your prejudices and mental pictures. If you can stay with your own *experience* of him or her, share the things that are important to you and the reasons why, then you will be able to discuss religion without creating a battle zone every time. When I asked couples who were happy and satisfied with the quality of their marriage how they let their partner know what was important to them, they inevitably had the same answer: "I just tell him (or her) . . . as often as I can."

Heather, twenty-six, who was raised as an Evangelical Christian, said it simply and well when, in speaking of her relationship with Eddie (who is twenty-eight and Jewish), she said, "You have to be willing to accept and try to understand the other. There are differences between religions and values, but they go together to make a whole relationship. The only way that you can *really* be supportive of each other in the relationship is to communicate in every way that you can exactly what and how you feel. That is simply a sign of trust, faith, and respect."

Andy, a Congregationalist, and Michelle, a Jew, had a similar outlook on keeping their marriage happy and satisfied. Michelle said, "We make sure that the other is aware of what is important to us and how we feel through vigorous discussions about everything. We talk about *everything,* just to make sure that we remember that you can't read the other's mind."

Andy continued, "Yes, we often disagree about things, but we either compromise one way or the other, or we take the most reasoned approach to the problem. Rather than simply argue about things, we try to share what we feel, and why we feel that way. It's hard to argue with someone's feelings."

Yes, it *is* hard to argue with someone's feelings without denigrating them. That is why the best strategy for open and supportive communication is simply to focus on your own feelings, rather than arguing whether or not your partner's feelings make sense to you. As Michelle summed it up, "The most important thing is to talk to each other, air your feelings, and let each do what he or she needs to do. Communicating with each other, not keeping things inside, is the crucial component of a successful relationship."

Nonconfrontational Conversations

Although communication is certainly the key to successfully discussing religion together in a mutually supportive relationship, it takes more than simply *talking* with one another to communicate effectively. Often couples with the best intentions end up hurting each other's feelings, alienating one another, and creating more misunderstanding than they had before they began.

There are several strategies for effective communication that are important to keep in mind. First, remember that self-disclosure is one of the best ways for diffusing potential arguments. Even the most heated disagreement can be instantly derailed ninety-nine percent of the time with the use of this simple technique.

Imagine you and your partner are in the middle of a loud and unpleasant argument over whether you will raise potential children in one religion or both. As the disagreement gets increasingly unpleasant, you suddenly realize that both of you are simply venting frustrations and hostility, and not even really listening to each other's point of view. Make a personal statement about how you *feel,* totally unconnected to the alleged subject of the conversation. "All of a sudden I feel very frightened and scared. I feel like I'm out of touch with the most important thing in my life, which is you and our relationship. I feel like I used to when I was a little girl/boy at home, alone and frightened. Would you just hold me for a minute and not say anything?"

That kind of interjection is guaranteed to almost always cut off all the arguments, and refocus both of you on how you feel, and the importance of your relationship. Asking to be held or touched is also a good way to reconnect physically with your partner. Most of the time when you argue you begin to move *physically* as well as emotionally apart from each other, and the simple act of touching can often re-center both of you on your relationship and your love.

Self-disclosure can take many forms. It not only involves sharing your emotions with your partner, but can also focus on feelings about your own religion that are less than totally positive.

Often the simple fact that they are involved with someone of another religion is enough to make some feel that it is their responsibility to defend their own religion, even aspects about which they have either totally neutral feelings, or have actually been negative about in the past.

Letting your partner know that you too don't agree with, believe in, or even understand everything that comes along with your own religion will make it much easier for the two of you to discuss aspects of the other's religion that you either don't understand or don't like. This is perhaps the *most* effective use of self-disclosure—taking the initiative when it comes to admitting that there are aspects of your own religion that you would have designed differently, if it were up to you.

Arguing Above the Belt

Arguing above the belt is primarily an exercise in self-discipline. It is the ability to argue assertively and forcefully with the one you love, without allowing yourself to sink to the level of ethnic/ religious/racial slurs. Taking potshots at your partner's religion or religious beliefs can only erode the quality of your relationship and create resentments that can last a lifetime.

An ancient book of Jewish wisdom teaches that words are like the arrow sent forth from the bow—once it lets loose it can never be brought back, and you are never certain where or who it will hurt. The sting may subside, but the ache often lingers forever. People tend to remember painful things that others say to them, and they can add up to form a foundation of distrust and discomfort.

The issue is one of respect: If you truly respect the one you love, you will protect their dignity, and the dignity of their religious beliefs and practices, even in the heat of argument. You are never so carried away by emotion that you simply don't know what you are doing. If you are, you should consider getting some therapy. Most of us are always in control of ourselves at some level, even if it is deep, and it is important to be responsible for our words and actions, and the impact that they have on others.

Standing in the Other's Shoes

It is often much easier for us to criticize someone than it is to take the time to imagine what the world must look like from their point of view. A third technique for effective communication follows the advice given in practically every religious system that I know—don't judge your neighbor until you have stood in his/her shoes.

Perhaps one of the most valuable traits you can ever cultivate is the ability to empathize with another person. It is a gift worth its weight in gold.

You can practice with your partner. Take turns describing how she/he might feel or think about a given situation or circumstance, then compare notes to find out how accurate you have been. Imagine that *you* had grown up with the same set of circumstances that your partner has—the same parents, siblings, schooling, background, homelife, religious experiences—and you will be quick to realize if all that were true, you would probably think and feel much the same way that your partner does today.

Eddie and Heather work hard at cultivating this skill with each other. Eddie said, "I'd help articulate the differences in our backgrounds as well as I could see them, and then try to feel how *she* might be feeling. I think that helped create a sense of togetherness in our relationship, like we were really in this together."

"It's probably even more true for him than for me," Heather interjected. "He was always by my side every step of the way from the beginning—being helpful and sympathetic to my feelings."

I have listened time and again as interfaith couples have told me how they kept stepping on each other's feelings without meaning to, especially in the beginning of their relationship. "At first we hurt each other a lot without knowing it," Eddie told me. "We'd say things innocently that would hurt the other's feelings because we just didn't know any better. But we kept saying 'That hurt me' to each other and eventually we have all but eliminated it."

Eddie and Heather have inadvertently stumbled upon the absolute best solution to this problem: When your partner says something that hurts you, simply say "That hurt me" as often as it takes to learn from direct trial and error experience what it is that hurts your feelings, and what doesn't. It is a strategy based on mutual trust and love and involves the willingness to perceive the other as a loving, caring, nurturing, supportive, struggling person, who truly *wants* to learn about us and our world view, and who makes mistakes without malice.

The most attuned lovers inadvertently hurt each other's feelings. If you are in doubt as to whether something you are about to say might push a sensitive emotional button in your partner, ask them in advance. Try a simple statement to the effect that you don't want to say anything that might hurt them, but since you were raised differently you know that words don't always have the same associations for the two of you, so please say something if something is upsetting them. You'd be amazed at how far that can go to desensitize your conversations.

Another strategy which others have used to their great satisfaction in many cases is a version of "What they don't know won't hurt them." Ruth and Walter are a perfect example of this process in action. "It's very simple really," Ruth told me. "I just don't tell Walter about certain things that happen, and he does the same with me, if we think it will hurt the other. I believe in being honest, but I try to protect him from things that I think would hurt his feelings."

"Yes," Walter agreed, "if I hear someone say something that I think will be uncomfortable or unpleasant for Ruth to hear, I just choose not to share it. I wouldn't lie to her, and if she asked me I would tell whatever I knew about anything or anyone since *she* is my first priority in life. But at the same time, I choose not to go out of my way to share something with her that would only upset her and can have no positive consequences for anyone if she hears about it."

Indeed, many couples have chosen this as the path of least resistance. It does work for many, but there is a risk involved as well. Never forget that everything you do within the context of your relationship adds one more piece to the total picture of what your relationship is all about. The more experiences you have of not being totally honest with your partner, or of withholding information, the more you may be setting up expectations of your behavior that include lack of honesty and forthrightness.

Protecting the quality and character of your relationship should always be the top priority. You therefore must strike a balance between the competing demands of openness and honesty in communication, and concern over hurting the feelings of the one you love.

One of the major potential problems in interfaith relationships stems from the very different world views that people from different religious backgrounds have. Each religious community has its own rules and ways of celebrating special moments in life. Even in same-faith marriages, one person feels that the way *he* celebrated Christmas (the kind of food they ate, whether they

opened presents in the morning or evening, etc.) is the *right* way
to celebrate, and his partner feels that *her* childhood experiences
represent the right way. Imagine how easy it is for this same
principle to operate in interfaith relationships!

The inevitable result of just such a biased judgment leads to
what I call the right/wrong trap. It is the not uncommon situation
where the way you were raised seems "right" to you, and the way
your partner was raised seems "wrong."

For example, thirty-eight-year-old Terri told me, "Jim and I used
to argue all the time about the stupidest things. It's so easy to
forget that you both come from very different backgrounds and
don't have the same childhood memories and experiences. Most
of the time our arguments would be about everyday things like
going out to restaurants or staying home.

"I used to get upset with Jim because I expected that every
Sunday we would go out to dinner, and he liked to eat at home.
When I grew up in my Jewish family from New York, it was
practically a religious ritual with everyone I knew that Sunday
night was out-with-the-family-to-the-Chinese-restaurant night.

"Now I know that this sounds silly, but it was one of my favorite
childhood memories, and I always looked forward to the time
when I would be an adult with my own family, and we would go
out for *our* Sunday night dinners."

"I grew up with exactly the opposite experience," Jim added.
"My childhood was filled with memories of my father's not being
around very much because he had a job that kept him away from
home several days a week on the road. For me, the most wonderful time of the week was Sunday night dinner, when my whole
family would be together at home. It made me feel like I was a
normal kid with a normal family that sits down at a dinner table
and eats together. I loved it and used to think about how it would
be when I grew up and had my own family sitting together at home
every Sunday night around the dinner table."

"It must have taken us almost a year to finally figure all that
out," Terri mused. "One day after arguing about Sunday dinners
in or out for month after month and getting nowhere, suddenly Jim
in a fit of frustration blurted out, 'You're ruining all my childhood
fantasies,' and it stopped me cold in my tracks.

"I remember just sitting there for a long moment, totally absorbing what he had said, realizing for the first time that *his* fantasies and *my* fantasies were totally different, and that they were behind all our arguments over dinner. It was like a ray of light from heaven, and I burst out laughing.

"After that, we sat around for a long time sharing our childhood pictures of what-my-life-will-be-like-when-I-grow-up and learned so many wonderful and interesting things about each other that cleared up lots of misunderstandings that we had had all along without even knowing."

I loved listening to Jim and Terri talk about how they broke through the unconscious barriers of childhood fantasy that had haunted their relationship, for I knew how often such simple and unacknowledged thoughts undermine a couple's ability to understand each other and truly communicate.

The right/wrong trap is primarily a result of these childhood images of what is right, what is wrong, what is proper and what is improper when it comes to behavior, rituals, celebrations, and even normal everyday life activities. To the extent that you are aware that they are operating like hidden mental guides in your life, you can expose them to the light of adult reason and discussion, and they instantly lose most of their power over you.

Here, once again, the key is open communication with one another. It rests on the assumption that each truly loves and wants to understand all there is to know about the other, so as to create a stronger, more supportive, and mutually satisfying relationship.

Monica, forty-three, described her relationship in exactly these terms when she said, "We are constantly reminding ourselves that there is no right and wrong, black or white. Take the issue of Christ for example. I can't tell Bill that Christ was the Savior, it's my own belief. You have to recognize that there are no clear-cut rights and wrongs either way. It has a lot to do with the respect that you have for other people and their beliefs, especially for your spouse."

Respect must be the foundation of any successful relationship. Having respect for the one you love makes it easier to break through the childhood barriers that exist for both of you, and to understand the role that unconscious stereotypes play in the attitudes and perceptions that lie beneath many of the arguments and disagreements that can plague interfaith relationships.

Understanding the Role of Stereotypes

Stereotypes of religious groups seem to be part and parcel of the experiences of many who have been involved with interfaith dating and marriage. These stereotypes often appear as if from nowhere, and when examined usually have their origin in one or two isolated encounters with a member of another religious group. Be that as it may, once an individual has made a decision about the nature of "Jewish men" or "Catholic women," that image seems to stay with them for many years.

The stereotypes and images that individuals create often become almost an excuse for either being with or not being with members of a particular religion. One Jewish woman who was married to a Presbyterian man told me that she could never have married a Jewish man because "Jewish men all want to be mothered. I don't know what their problem is, but with a Christian man you know who wears the pants in the family."

The impact of family upbringing and of the role models that are present in the formative years of an individual's life seems to go unnoticed by the vast majority of the couples with whom I meet. Most honestly believe that the particular stereotype that they hold is simply the objective fact about that group. It often surprises them greatly to learn that others have a totally opposite view of the same group. Indeed, people in many marriages must begin by overcoming stereotypes that have been an integral part of their youth or upbringing.

The existence of stereotypes alone is not a problem; it is how one deals with the reality of their presence that separates successful from unsuccessful relationships.

Sharing stereotypes of each other is a creative approach to a troublesome situation. When done in a loving, open way it can be yet another drawing-together experience. It is an opportunity to demonstrate among other things your trust in your partner. Simply being willing to share what you know to be prejudices and generalizations about the other is a way of saying "I trust you with my feelings. I trust that you will know I love you and that I can share even potentially embarrassing things with you and it will be safe." It is one way of making sure that those stereotypes do *not* create a problem between you. Either you let these prejudices control your attitudes, your behavior towards your partner, and therefore in a real way control your life, or *you* control *them*.

Often I have been told that being in a relationship with someone of a different background has been a powerful learning experience filled with personal growth and the constant challenge of new discovery.

Deidre was a perfect example of this. She was twenty-one, Protestant, married to a forty-one-year-old Jewish man. She admitted to me that "being married to a Jewish person has been an eye-opening experience for me. I have grown much more sensitive and aware of the feelings of the Jews as a people, their concerns regarding anti-Semitism and the prejudice in the world around us, than I ever would have, had I not married Aron.

"This has been a big difference for me and an important one as well. It has added a new dimension to my life and my perceptions of the world in which we live. In a way, it is an opportunity to overcome childhood stereotypes, to gain a totally new perspective on life, to discover things about myself and others that I never thought of before, and to expand my ability to identify and empathize with others."

An interesting psychological aspect of the negative stereotypes that individuals hold about other groups is that they are often primarily directed toward members of the opposite sex in *their own* religious group. For example, Carol, who is Protestant, told me that "Protestant men don't have ambition and drive like Jewish men do." Susan, who is Jewish, said, "Jewish men are too concerned about pleasing their parents and never let go of the apron strings." Vincent, who is Catholic, told me, "Catholic girls are too uptight about things and are always feeling guilty about everything just because it's fun to do"; and David, who is Jewish, said, "Jewish girls are too demanding. They are perfectionists and are always nagging you to do better than you did. Who wants to feel like you never quite measure up?"

Some of the images that people have of each other would be

funny, if they weren't depressing. When Carol was raised as a strict Lutheran in the Midwest, she didn't know any Jews. She did however know two things about them: one, they were going to hell, and two, they had horns!

Carol met Howard in a class during her first year of college in California. On their first date, she actually spent the entire night feeling his head to try and find the horns. She told me she had never been so embarrassed in her life as when he realized what she was doing and *she* realized how foolish that negative stereotype truly was.

In an interfaith relationship, the various stereotypes that exist can either be a source of divisiveness or they can actually serve as a bonding force between the couple. As with every relationship, it is important for the couple in an interfaith marriage to share a common set of beliefs about their own place within the greater family and social order.

Every couple needs to feel that they have their own world, a world that is special to the two of them. It is a world of the shared experiences of their relationship, and the secrets that they share with only each other. It is a composite of the mutually shared moments, stories, attitudes and interpretations of their experiences that gives them the knowledge that their relationship is inviolate.

When a relationship becomes a sanctuary from the stresses and tensions of the outside world, then the common myths and beliefs about each other's religion can simply be a part of that bond of shared beliefs and experiences that strengthens the relationship itself. When Carol and Howard got over their initial embarrassment at Carol's search for Howard's horns, it became a lifelong bonding secret between them, giving them many moments of shared laughter and smiles.

Each interfaith relationship can benefit from a sharing of the stereotypes that each partner has of the other. It is only when these go unexpressed yet continue to inform and direct your thoughts and actions that they become divisive and dangerous to your relationship.

The Importance of Clarifying Your Own Beliefs

There are many paths to religious self-discovery and awareness. It is up to each individual, working alone and as a team within the marriage or relationship, to find the path that will work the best for them. It is not important which path you eventually choose, what *is* important is to choose.

It is important to take the time prior to making the decision to marry to confront your own beliefs, feelings, needs, and priorities with regard to religion in general, and your own religious background in particular. Do it for yourself, as a gift of trust and integrity to your partner, and for the ultimate inner strength and peace of mind that comes from a significant act of personal courage and honesty. When you do that, discovering your own religious feelings becomes an opportunity for personal growth, satisfaction, and joy, which is, after all, what life is all about.

This process can be a stressful experience within the context of an interfaith relationship. The consequences may be the strengthening of the relationship, the conversion to the religion of your partner, the creation of a workable compromise that satisfies the needs of both partners, or the dissolution of the relationship itself.

If you need help with this process, whether from a minister, rabbi, therapist, friend, support group, sibling, or parent, be courageous enough to seek it out. It is the only life you know you will live, so it's up to you to make the most out of it.

So, how do you go about discovering what it is that is important to you with regard to religion? There are numerous paths to the same goal, but let's look at how one couple went about their search together.

Ed (twenty-eight, Jewish) and Nancy (twenty-seven, Protestant) met in a sushi bar. They both lived in a suburb of Chicago and frequented the same neighborhood stores, restaurants, and theaters, which helped them feel an immediate sense of rapport. Their life-styles were basically the same, and they enjoyed going to the same movies and plays, listening to similar music, and obviously eating the same foods.

One evening, after they had been going out for several months,

Ed turned to Nancy as they were on their way out to dinner and asked, "How would you like to come with me to High Holiday services next week?"

Nancy was a bit surprised since she had never had a single conversation with Ed involving religion or religious practice before. "I've never been to one," she replied. "When is it, what is it, and where is it?"

"Next Thursday night, it's the Jewish New Year service, and it's at my parents' temple. They would love to have you come along, and since I still go with them every year, I thought it would be an interesting experience for you. Besides, I'd have a much better time if you were there."

Nancy responded, "I'm not so sure I would be comfortable. I wouldn't have any idea what to do once I'm there, and I'd probably do something to embarrass you or your family. Besides, the thought of going to services with your family is too scary."

"Ok," Ed countered, "then I don't think I'll go this year either. I don't want to do anything that is going to make you uncomfortable. This relationship is going too well; I don't want to blow it."

Well, as you might imagine, that was not the end of the conversation. Nancy began to feel guilty, as if she were responsible for coming between Ed and his parents. She also was afraid that by not going she was insulting his family, and that if this relationship did turn into something more serious, she would have totally alienated Ed's mother and father.

Ed, on the other hand, had created a no-win situation for himself. He had used an important religious event as the time to first introduce the idea of Nancy's participating in anything Jewish with him and his family, and found himself having made a commitment out loud to Nancy that for "her sake" he too would skip High Holiday services with his family, which he realized he didn't really want to do.

It was at this point that they showed up in my office one Sunday afternoon. "I'm not sure what happened," Ed began, "but we need your help in straightening out a delicate situation."

"I feel terrible," Nancy interjected. "Without doing a thing, I feel like *I'm* the bad guy in this scenario, as if I'm wrecking some important religious occasion for Ed and his parents. I don't like being in this position."

"I don't like it either," Ed continued. "I suppose I must have started it all when I asked Nancy if she wanted to come to High Holiday services with me and my family, and she declined the offer. How do I get out of this mess without hurting someone's feelings, or worse?"

My approach with the two of them was fairly simple. I saw it as a perfect opportunity for them to begin addressing the underlying questions regarding the role and importance of religion in their lives, so I began asking them the kind of questions that I believe every couple should address.

I gave each of them a piece of paper and asked them to complete the following sentences:

1. When I think of my religion _____.
2. When I don't celebrate a holiday, I feel _____.
3. As a child, religion to me was _____.
4. My favorite religious experience was _____.
5. The thing that makes me most uncomfortable about my boy/ girlfriend's religion is _____.
6. The thing I like least about my own religion is _____.
7. If it were up to me, our involvement with my religion _____.
8. If I had the nerve, I would tell my boy/girlfriend _____.
9. When I think about Jesus, I feel _____.
10. If I never had anything to do with religion again _____.

When they finished these ten starter questions, I collected their responses and used them to carry on a discussion that allowed them to focus on those elements of their own religion that they liked, those they didn't like, and how they felt about their partner's religion. I pointed out that it was normal to have anxieties about stepping into a religious situation that they had never experienced before. Most of us don't like surprises because we are secretly afraid of being embarrassed and feeling foolish.

Nancy laughed at that point and admitted that the primary reason she had declined Ed's offer in the first place was simply fear of looking and feeling like a fool. "What do you think it would take to prepare you enough in advance so that you would feel comfortable going?" I asked.

She thought it over and then replied, "Well, if Ed told me everything that was going to happen while I was there, showed me the books they use in the service, and explained what I will have to do before I get there, I would probably feel comfortable enough to go."

"You're kidding!" Ed exclaimed. "That's easy. I can do that in a few minutes. Actually, it's all pretty boring anyway; you mostly just sit and listen to the rabbi talk and the cantor and choir sing."

After we had resolved that problem, I turned to the more fundamental issues of their relationship. Clarifying what is important takes honesty, and the way Ed had handled it was a good lesson in what happens when you aren't really honest with yourself. The issue ultimately comes back to the importance of good communication skills. Particularly in the area of religious theology, it is important to share that which you believe with the one you love. Often your true religious feelings are most evident while you are celebrating a holiday or religious ritual, whether yours or someone else's. This is the best time to get in touch with the emotions that are stimulated by the candles on the table, the words of a prayer, the smell of the tree, the music of a service.

Next, look beyond your initial emotional reactions. When someone says, "I don't believe in heaven and hell; when you die that's simply it; there is nothing else," pay attention to what you feel, the thoughts that go through your mind. Such self-conscious thinking can help you to identify those beliefs that are important to you, and those that are simply rote regurgitation of childhood Sunday school programming.

Talk with your partner about their beliefs concerning sin and punishment, the need for forgiveness from God, the existence of a God who created the universe and responds to the prayers of human beings, life after death, and other significant religious beliefs. Sharing your inner beliefs and faith is another bonding experience for many, even when there isn't total agreement in the beliefs themselves.

Sometimes the discovery of your own fundamental religious beliefs comes about as the direct result of a supportive dialogue with someone you love. It can happen simply by putting yourself in an environment that is conducive to philosophical speculation and discussion. Such was the case with Richard, who was born to a practicing Conservative Jewish family, and who married a woman from a mainstream Protestant midwestern background.

Richard sees himself as a sort of amateur philosopher: his religious thinking was clarified through a conscious process of taking classes in philosophy and comparative religion at his local college. He looks at religion from the perspective of one who feels his life is in his hands, not in the hands of an all-powerful supernatural being. "I believe that religion is there to serve us and not the other way around," he said.

"Yes, I did enjoy my Jewish upbringing and felt a sense of Jewish identity as a child. But still, Judaism, like any religion, is there to help us with guidelines for acting in a way that will bring a better world into being. That can take place with anyone's religion. No one has a corner on the goodness or righteousness market—not Jews, not Catholics, Muslims, Buddhists, or what have you.

"I believe the most important thing is to be a good person, not to hurt others, to help them when you can, and do your best to bring peace into the world." Richard discovered that he actually felt much closer in religious theology to his wife, Lisa, than his Jewish upbringing would have suggested. This discovery also made it easier for Richard to discard many of the rituals, customs, and ceremonies of Judaism, and merge his life with Lisa into one that can best be described as "secular American Protestantism."

For Richard, discovering his own religious feelings was a process that included long discussions with Lisa, serious study of religions other than Judaism, and the willingness to confront honestly the level of his Jewish commitment. For others, the process of self-discovery takes place in a less structured, more informal way.

For some, clarifying their beliefs involves the willingness to accept that the person they love believes things that they don't. Howard and Carol came to a meeting of the minds on religious issues as they struggled to identify those areas of belief they held in common, and those which divided them. Howard told me, "I just can't understand how anyone can believe in Jesus," and Carol responded, "I know that he feels that way, so we just don't discuss it. We decided not to talk about religion at all anymore and have accepted the reality that he believes his way and I believe mine, and never the twain will meet. That's just the way it is."

I pointed out to them that it was that way because they had

chosen to make it that way, and as long as they didn't bring children into the picture, their individual beliefs could remain just that—individual beliefs. They knew, however, that as soon as they decided to have children, the entire realm of religious theology, what to teach their children, where to send them if anywhere for religious training, would have to be confronted. They were so afraid of what that might do to their relationship that they simply avoided all discussion of both religion *and* children.

Obviously, the likelihood was slim that they could keep up this avoidance forever, and I suggested to them that if they intended to be together for a long time, they owed it to each other to be honest with their needs and feelings. By the time they left my office, they had made a promise to each other (and to me) that they would take the next month to confront the differences between them. They were finally courageous enough to be willing to discover whether their differences were enough to prevent them from having a future together or not.

One of the easiest methods of clarification is to sit down with a blank piece of paper and write out a list of "I believe . . ." and "I don't believe . . ." statements. Think about your own religion and the religion of your partner as you write. Do your best to come up with at least ten statements for each category, and then sit and share your lists with each other.

The next step is to focus your statements on specific aspects of religion or religious beliefs and rituals. For example, you might write out statements that begin "When I think of my church I _____," "If I never went back to church/synagogue I _____," "The thing I enjoy most about church/synagogue is _____," and other statements that help clarify beliefs and feelings.

These are all simple techniques to facilitate communication and clarification. After you are in touch with how you feel as an adult about your religion and the religion of your partner, it is important to spend time together sharing your dreams for the future.

Perhaps the easiest way to examine your future (given the fact that we never really know how we will feel in the future) is to focus on possible children. Once again, by completing a few sentences that begin "I want my children to believe _____," and then sharing them with each other, you will focus on your own fantasies of religious child raising and have a better understanding of where you and your partner differ.

Religious tensions that develop between interfaith couples usually appear in a clash over religious ideology. The expression of this tension may in fact be focused on a specific religious event, but the underlying problem is usually one of differences in religious belief.

For example, John and Melony have discovered that although they agree on much when it comes to religious observance, and both feel that they share certain common religious values, there is one issue over which they seriously disagree.

John has discovered that his belief in Jesus is a very important part of his life. It is a constant frustration and source of separation between them that Melony, as a Jew, doesn't share that belief. Each holiday becomes filled with tension as they both bend over backward not to offend the other with their various religious symbols and rituals.

As adults they can resolve relatively painlessly, for most adults are able to be tolerant of another's right to believe whatever he or she chooses. But, when it comes to children, to the many decisions regarding what they feel is important to pass on to the next generation, they run into a theological brick wall.

Neither of them will be happy if *their* child is taught the theology of the other. Neither would be satisfied to place the religious upbringing of their child in the hands of the other. It is so painfully clear to them that this dilemma has no solution that they are resigned to an exclusively adult relationship, knowing that when they do want to have children, they will both want it to be with someone whose beliefs are consistent with their own.

Practical Versus Philosophical— Belief Versus Action

Each of us experiences and expresses our own particular religion on two basic levels, which I like to call practical and philosophical.

Practical refers to the everyday expression of one's religion in the rituals, holidays, and celebrations that are participated in on a daily, monthly, or annual basis. Most of us relate to our respective religion on this practical level most of the time. In fact, to most of us, these daily activities *are* our religion, and to the extent that another is willing to join with us in these various celebrations and rituals, we see no religious conflict between us at all.

Most of the time we simply live our lives, incorporating into them some small measure of celebration and ritual, and consider that to be our form of religious practice. Tensions arise in interfaith relationships when the practical and the philosophical come into conflict.

Philosophical refers to the underlying religious principles, attitudes about the nature of human beings, sin, salvation, God, heaven and hell, death and afterlife, that are at the foundation of a given religious way of life. In truth, many adherents of a particular religion would be at a loss to clearly and accurately describe what these various philosophical underpinnings are in the first place.

The confluence of practical and philosophical can be devastating. Interfaith couples generally negotiate their relationship on the level of the practical, with the specific decisions relating to which holidays they will celebrate, with whom, and in what manner. These decisions seem to constitute a satisfactory accommodation between the two religious backgrounds, and the couple generally feel that they have successfully blended their respective traditions together when such decisions are made.

The problem that must be addressed is that most religious conflicts arise primarily in the area of philosophy, and less profoundly on the practical level. It is crucial for you to face these issues of philosophy squarely so that you don't end up years into a marriage before realizing that there are hopeless philosophical differences that divide you from the one you love. Take every opportunity that you have to share your feelings about religion and its role in your life and future *before* you are feeling pressured to make a decision about marriage.

Give yourself and the one you love the most important gift you can—the gift of truth and honesty. Then you will know that your life is turning out the way it is supposed to, for *you* are creating it that way.

Chapter IV

SHOULD WE
GET MARRIED?

"If couples aren't willing to face realistically the problems of their marriage, they shouldn't get married in the first place."

—Bill, interfaith married four years

When working with couples who are about to get married, at some point during our session together I always ask them what appears at first glance to be the rather simple, if not innocuous question, "Why are you getting married?"

Sometimes I hear "We are getting married because it's time to settle down." Or, "Well, I'm X years old and it's time to start a family." Too many couples have too many "reasons" for getting married. Too many get married, believe it or not, simply because somebody actually *asked* them. Too many despair of ever finding or creating a relationship of mutual love, trust, empathy, support, and understanding with another human being. Much to my chagrin, it is actually the *minority* of couples who, when asked, "Why are you getting married?" simply reply, "We love each other and want to spend our lives together." The minority!

The Best Reason for Getting Married

To my mind, there is basically only one "good" reason for getting married. That one reason, simply put, is *love*. When couples get married for all the other reasons to which they admit, they are choosing a relationship that is based primarily on something *other* than simply their feelings for the one they are marrying.

Surprising as it may sound, some people get married in order to *end* a relationship! Such a couple were Bea and Randy.

I met them at the reception following an interfaith wedding at which I officiated. Randy, hearing that I was writing a book on interfaith marriage, found me in the crowd and began sharing his personal story with me. He and Bea had been married for just over a year, but had been together off and on for over five years.

Their story is sadly typical of so many who become trapped inside the tangled web of a relationship they know is wrong for them, but somehow can't find the door that will lead them out. Randy and Bea had spent much of their courtship arguing about their families. He believed that she grew up in a clannish, overly protective Jewish family, and she saw his Protestant family as mildly prejudiced and narrow-minded.

They were constantly in and out of each other's arms, fighting, then making up again. Their relationship was more like an addiction than anything else, and Randy told me they got increasingly frustrated at the state of limbo in which they lived.

They finally decided that they had to either break it off for good or make the commitment to each other and get married. As with so many other couples in their situation, Randy and Bea chose to let the internal momentum of their years of being together lead them down the aisle to marriage.

After only a year of marriage, they were in the process of separating from each other and knew that their relationship was over for good. It is sad how many people end up just like Randy and Bea. Time and again I have spoken to couples who have become so entangled in a relationship for so long that they feel compelled to carry it to its ultimate conclusion—marriage. Only then did they feel free to say to themselves and each other that they had given it their "best shot," that they had done all they could for the relationship and therefore were able to get divorced and finally do what they couldn't do before—end it.

When a couple marry because they both feel it is time to start a family, the child or children-to-be are the "real" reason for the marriage. The relationship is simply a vehicle for carrying out their intended purpose. Too many couples have come to see me on the way to their divorce proceedings having realized after a number of years (and sometimes a number of children) that there is very little in terms of a real, nurturing, and fulfilling relationship between them.

Each will of course fight for custody of the children, since *they* are the reason the couple subjected themselves to the marriage in the first place. But the relationship itself long ago faded from romance to indifference as each drifted farther and farther away from the other. Unfortunately, the *children* are the ones who suffer the most.

Children are brought into this world without the ability to choose their parents. In the truest sense of the word, they become the innocent victims of the immature and unthinking life decisions that their parents have made.

When two adults marry each other primarily as a means to procreation, it is in most cases a form of egotism and narcissism. How many children have been brought into this world as a human sacrifice on the altar of self-indulgence and the need to achieve some form of immortality? How many innocent children have been brought into the world primarily for the purpose of providing an emotionally needy adult someone with whom they can experience unconditional love?

Sadly, it is a daily occurrence, and one which I see as a major underlying cause of divorce today. It happens in marriages of all kinds, between and within all faiths, but it is an even more sensitive issue for interfaith marriages. As you can imagine, interfaith marriages are subject to built-in stresses and strains that same-faith marriages do not necessarily have to face.

All the more reason to do whatever is in your power to create a relationship based on mutual love, caring, trust, and support before you make the decision to consummate that relationship in marriage.

Recent studies indicate that interfaith marriages fail at up to six times the rate of same-faith marriages. Choosing a mate, a partner with whom to share your life, your dreams, and your struggles is difficult under the best of circumstances. When different religious and cultural backgrounds are thrown into the hopper, it compounds the risks and increases the possibility of a breakdown in the relationship.

Get married for the right reasons. Get married because you love your partner, because you can't imagine spending your life without them, because you have discovered in them a soul mate who complements the inner core of your own true spirit.

How to Talk About Marriage

In working with couples over the years I have found three concrete steps for talking effectively about marriage. They are (1) sharing your real fears, (2) asking the right questions, and (3) listing priorities.

The idea is simply to create as many strategies as possible for clarifying the aspects of your own religious background that are important to you *before* you make the commitment to marriage. It will help insure that when you do decide to get married, you both will know that you have been open and honest with each other about your religious needs and fears, thereby eliminating one of the major stumbling blocks to successful interfaith relationships.

When Kurt and Lynne first came to see me they were deciding whether or not to get married, in spite of the fact that she was Jewish and he was raised as a Catholic. They had lived together for two years, seemed to share basic values and ideas about the kind of life they wanted to live, yet were mature enough to realize that there were other considerations. Having heard that I was involved in the issue of interfaith marriage, they sought me out for counseling and suggestions.

The first thing I had them share with each other were the fears that they both secretly had about each other in particular and interfaith marriage in general. "I guess what I am really most afraid of is that Kurt will want to have my children baptized," Lynne finally said, after much probing on my part. "There is so much about the Catholic religion that seems irrational and almost spooky to me that I think I would really be upset if Kurt suddenly became a closet believer with a secret missionary fervor to save the immortal souls of me and my children.

"I know it sounds kind of silly to worry about it, especially since in the two years we have been living together, and the year before that in which we were dating, he never once even mentioned a desire to go to church or basically expressed any belief in Jesus as the Savior or any of that stuff. But I know that deep down inside I do have that fear."

Kurt, hearing this for the first time, realized that he hadn't really given the subject much thought. As with many people who were raised in Catholic families and as adults got involved in interfaith relationships, he hadn't been to Mass since he was about fourteen. He had drifted away from the Church, feeling that it wasn't particularly relevant to his contemporary life.

Now that the issue had come up, however, he said that to be perfectly honest about it he would have to give some serious thought to just what it was he *did* feel about baptism. I asked him if he thought that the souls of babies would end up suspended in some kind of spiritual limbo if they died before being baptized. "I suppose I did believe that at one time in my life," he responded, "but now that I consider the subject as an adult who has been away from it for a long time, I don't really believe that anymore. In fact, I believe that if there is a heaven at all (which I'm not really sure of since there is no way for me to know until I die), it must be available to all people who are good at heart, and not just Catholics or Baptists or Jews or Muslims."

Lynne was relieved to hear Kurt's response, and once again I marveled at how they had never discussed this fear of hers during all the years of their relationship.

When I have discussed the issue of talking about your marriage in advance with interfaith couples who have been successful in their marriages over many years, they inevitably told me the same things. Melony and John are thirty-six and forty-one, respectively, and have been married for sixteen years. John is Lutheran and Melony is Jewish. "Basically, you have to be honest with each other about how you feel," said Melony. "Particularly when it comes to religion and your own beliefs, you can't afford to gloss over them as if they don't matter to your future compatibility and happiness. Sometimes people say anything just to get married and don't discuss their true feelings. You really need to be blunt about how you feel about your religion and what is important to you, otherwise how will your potential marriage partner ever know?"

"It would be a mistake to get married thinking that everything will just work out," John added. "You need to take the time to decide if you really want to spend your life with this person given the religion they are from and their personal beliefs and needs. The only way you can do that is if you are honest with each other about the things you believe *and* the things you are afraid of that the other person might believe. Then you can enter a marriage as we did, having eliminated our secret fears in advance."

Sometimes the fears aren't really about the religion of your partner per se, but have to do with the problem of integrating into another's family system. Heather's biggest fear before and during the early stages of her marriage to Eddie was that she would remain an "outsider" forever as far as his family was concerned.

"Eddie has such a close-knit family that is always doing things together: sharing holidays, dinners each week, special events, and lots of Jewish celebrations of different kinds. As a *born-again* Christian I was afraid that they would never let me in. I remember thinking to myself for the longest time, 'How am I ever going to get *in* there?'

"What finally helped the most was the willingness to share this fear with Eddie. He was surprised that I felt that way, naturally, since it had never occurred to him that I could possibly feel uncomfortable or ill at ease with his warm, loving, open family— at least that's how *he* saw them.

"After I told him that I was scared I'd never fit in and be accepted, he was great. He helped a lot by making sure that I understood it wasn't something personal, just the natural fear that comes with trying to break into a family that has been together with all their shared experiences for so many years. He supported me all the way and made sure that I was included in everything.

"He also made sure that everything was always clear to me, explaining every aspect of the family holidays and celebrations and encouraging his family to do the same, which they did. With his encouragement, his entire family began to see 'making Heather a part of the family' as one of their major challenges of life, and it became fun for me instead of scary.

"Now that I do feel accepted and a part of everything, I love it, and it really feels great. But it never would have happened if I wasn't willing to share my fears with him from the start."

"We tried very hard to avoid hurt feelings and later pressures by discussing everything up front," Eddie commented. "Our marriage is a hundred times stronger than it might have been, because we were willing to make sure that there were no hidden fears and anxieties about each other's religion, beliefs, and practices that were left unexamined before we decided to actually get married."

The second important strategy for talking about marriage beforehand is to make sure that you ask the right questions of each other. Here are a few that I have found useful with interfaith couples:

1. What is the most important part of your religion to you?
2. When you hear the word Jew/Catholic/Lutheran (etc.), what do you think of?
3. What are you most afraid of about marrying a ———?
4. What is the importance of baptism to you?
5. How would you feel if your children weren't raised in your religion?
6. How would you feel if you heard your children telling someone that they were the religion of your spouse?
7. What is your biggest anxiety about your potential spouse's family?
8. What activity with your spouse and his/her family produces the most anxiety in you?
9. What is your favorite holiday and why?
10. What do you like the least about your partner's religion?

I'm sure you can think of many more that will help in the process of clarifying your religious values with each other. The idea is simply to do whatever you can to make sure that you are willing to discuss these issues *before* you make the decision to get married. It is always harder to change your mind after telling the world you are getting married than it is simply not to make that decision in the first place.

The third suggestion for discussing marriage beforehand is to set aside some time and go through a process of listing priorities with each other. This can be as simple as taking a piece of paper, numbering down the left margin from 1 to 10, then listing from most to least important those aspects of your own religion that you expect to continue as a part of your life.

After you have made your lists, share them with each other, explain anything that isn't clear or about which your partner has questions, and you will probably be surprised at how much this simple exercise reveals.

One of the issues that interfaith couples struggle with the most is the question of what decisions they need to make prior to actually getting married. Even though I am a rabbi and religion is my daily occupation, I counsel interfaith couples that marriage between partners from different religious backgrounds is one of those areas of life in which too much faith can really be a dangerous thing.

In addition to decisions about the kind of wedding ceremony itself, there are two fundamental areas of your relationship that I believe are crucial to discuss and make decisions about *prior* to marriage. The first is your expectations of each other as husband and wife, father and mother, and religious partner, and the second is the question of having and raising children.

These issues are significant ones and can create major conflicts in your relationship and your life if they are not resolved satisfactorily. Too often I have seen couples rush into marriage certain that love will conquer all, determined to avoid conflict and disagreement at all costs, to the extent that they have consciously avoided discussing any of these issues because they fear that they might be sources of discontent or disagreement.

The relationships that are the most successful are usually those in which both partners recognized the need to discuss important areas of future life-style and child raising before the marriage vows were uttered. As they look back on the choices they made, and the discussions that they forced each other to have, many such couples credit the success of their marriage to these very discussions and decisions.

Bill, Jewish and forty-five, married for four years to Monica, Catholic and forty-three, certainly felt that way. Bill told me, "We discussed all the issues we could think of before we got married. I think we discussed as much as we possibly could about everything. Since we have been married, the only real problem has been my ex-wife, and there's nothing we can do about that one. Monica and I don't have arguments about religion at all because we already came to important agreements about these issues *before* we got married."

Monica added, "I think there are really a number of issues that an interfaith couple should discuss clearly before marriage. We dealt with basically four different areas in our discussions with each other:

"1. How to treat the holidays of the other.
   2. How to raise the children, what religion will they be, and why choose that one over the other?
   3. What happens to the religious training if there is a separation or divorce? If each parent gets one child in a divorce settlement, will they both be raised in the same faith?
   4. How do you communicate and what do you have to do to insure good communication with your in-laws and future relatives?"

Bobby, thirty-seven and Jewish, married for three years to Rita, thirty-five and Presbyterian, told me, "I would tell an interfaith couple to make decisions about their children. Even if you think that you aren't going to have any, you should decide what you will do if . . . You should decide upon how to work out family problems, and the importance of different family ties.

"Each person needs to be willing to give up some family ties for the relationship if necessary. With us there isn't any tension, but if there is, you need to have discussed in advance how you will handle it."

Walter, thirty-nine, a Southern Baptist, and Ruth, forty-two and Jewish, looked back and saw the ability to compromise as one of the single most important reasons for their successful ten-year marriage.

"One partner can't be convinced to do it the other's way," Ruth told me. "It must be a real agreement between them, a genuine compromise, otherwise the marriage wouldn't last anyway."

"I agree," Walter continued. "You really need to sit down like in a business meeting to decide your future. It's the same in all aspects of life. You need to be clear about your expectations and needs within the relationship and what is really important to you. Then you can communicate that to your partner, and he or she can agree or disagree to meet those needs. Either way you have a much better understanding of exactly what you are getting into before you actually get married."

Many marriages have foundered on the shoals of unrealistic expectations. Share with each other your own pictures of what it means to be a husband and a wife. Realize that each of us grows up with childhood fantasies of married life that are a combination of TV stereotypes (*All in the Family* meets *The Partridge Family*), fairy tales (Cinderella meets Prince Charming), popular music, advertising, and the general cultural background of our Western, Judeo-Christian society.

These childhood fantasies usually bear little resemblance to the reality of our relationships with the ones we love, but they continue to lurk in the cobwebbed corners of our minds, exerting just enough influence to cause a mild sensation of dis-ease when the man or woman we marry doesn't quite match up to our subconscious expectations. The best antidote for this condition is simply to bring the fantasy out into the open, since like all hobgoblins, it loses its power and simply disappears in the bright light of day.

Actually talk yourself through a typical day, week, month, or year, including the holidays you expect to celebrate, the events you expect to participate in, the kinds of activities that you expect to share, and see what your life might look like. I guarantee it will be a revealing conversation, and worth every minute that you spend with each other in the process.

Almost every successful interfaith couple with whom I have met felt that it was important to clear the air about raising children from the very start. Without doubt, the issue of how you will raise your children (assuming that you have any at all) is potentially the biggest relationship destroyer that exists.

It is amazing to me how many couples go out of their way to avoid any discussion of children at all prior to making the fateful decision to join their lives in marriage. It is as if they are hoping that if they simply ignore the issue, it will somehow magically disappear and they will never have to deal with it at all.

Often, they are aware that as single adults their different backgrounds present little conflict or problem between them, but that there is a serious possibility that discussing how they each imagine raising their children will sow dissension and discord in an otherwise harmonious relationship.

What I want to stress here is not the importance of one particular decision over another, one religion over another, or one method of religious child raising over another. The process of discussing the subject is more important than any particular decision that you might make together. Arthur, thirty-three and Protestant, had lived with Pam, thirty-eight and Jewish, for five years at the time of our interview. They had gotten married three months prior to our conversation and the issue of child raising had been a significant reason why they had waited so long.

"We just kept avoiding the subject all the time because we didn't want to create any tension or conflict in our relationship. Since we were getting along so well most of the time, and we really loved being with each other, neither of us was willing to cast the first stone, so to speak, and stir up the otherwise calm waters.

"I always knew somewhere in the back of my mind that we would have to face the children issue someday, but I was having such a good time as we were that I didn't want to rock the boat. Eventually it was Pam who broke the silence pact because she really wanted to get married and make this a permanent commitment. She had enough sense to realize, even if *I* resisted it, that we *had* to confront the children issue before we could ever really feel secure in a marriage decision."

"I spent years avoiding the subject just like Arthur," Pam continued. "But I kept feeling like we were only prolonging the inevitable, and that our relationship wasn't really sitting on a solid foundation as long as we kept away from talking about the implications of raising children in an interfaith family.

"I don't think that it is an easy issue for anyone to discuss, but it certainly is an important one. I was raised in a typical middle-class liberal Jewish family where going to temple was only mildly important. My parents were members for most of my childhood, but they didn't really stress religion or synagogue attendance very much.

"Still, my sister and I grew up with a strong sense of Jewish identity, knowing who we were, where we came from, and proud of being part of the Jewish community and Jewish history. I always knew that I wanted that same thing for my children, and when I fell in love with Arthur I did my best to bury my feelings for as long as possible."

"Fortunately for her," Arthur said, "*My* religious background was even weaker than hers. My family was never very religious, so I didn't have any strong feelings one way or the other about how we should raise our children. Pam didn't know that, of course; she imagined that I would want my kids to believe in Jesus and go to church, so she avoided it so she'd never have to find out."

"The important thing for any interfaith couple," Pam added, "is that eventually if you are going to have children, you have to consider their welfare along with your own. I think people should be kind to their children in advance, before they are born, and make sure that they will come into the world in a family that is secure, safe, together, and self-conscious when it comes to religious decisions."

So how then do you discuss in a positive and constructive way the issue of child raising before you get married, without having the relationship blow up in your face? You do it the same way you discuss everything else that is important to you—with calmness, sensitivity to the feelings of your partner, and a sense of trust that you both love each other and ultimately want what is best for both of you.

Use the same strategies that you have used to discuss other issues, and simply apply them to the subject of children. Take a piece of paper, number down the page from 1 to 10, then list in order of priority what you want most for your children down to what you want least.

Ask yourself and each other how you would feel if your child was a different religion from you, if he/she celebrated Christmas, had a Bar or Bat Mitzvah, was baptized or given a Hebrew name, went to church or synagogue, believed that Jesus was the divine Son of God or didn't, and see how you *feel* when you give the answers.

Your feelings are always the best indicator of whether you are being truthful and honest in your reactions to each other. They will let you know, if you are willing to pay attention to them, just how important each of these child-related religious questions are to you and guide you in making the correct decisions about getting married as well.

There is an old saying that change is the only constant in life. When it comes to relationships, marriage, and religion, change is indeed inevitable. The feelings that you have at fifteen may not be the same ones you have at twenty-five or thirty-five or forty-five. The problem is that you make decisions that affect the rest of your life at one stage of your development and often discover at a later stage that you have different needs and priorities.

Many couples have come to me in crisis after their first child is born because they made one decision together (in good faith) at the time of their marriage, and now have discovered that the arrival of the child evoked parenting responses that neither could have predicted in advance.

We will go into this in more detail in Chapter XI, but for now the important thing is to be willing to accept that your feelings, needs, and life-style choices do change over time.

Often it does take something dramatic or significant, like the birth of a child, to clarify what is really important to you about your religion. When that happens, you can experience frustration and even a sense of disappointment over not having been able to anticipate these new feelings in advance.

Don't be too hard on yourself, for your "true" feelings change over time whether you want them to or not. That is the way real human beings live in this imperfect world of ours, and it is important for your own peace of mind and mental health to accept it in yourself and your partner. What is unimportant today may become very important tomorrow, and what is desperately important today becomes something we smile at in disbelief ten years from now.

With all that said, it is still important to live in the present, make decisions with each other as *best and honestly* as you can, and simply know at the same time that there are no guarantees in life—especially in an interfaith relationship. The best thing you can do for yourself and your partner is to approach your marriage as a team—partners committed to dealing with the important issues together.

One of the best examples of a successful "team marriage" is that of Monica and Bill, whom we have met before. They are a model of a healthy, open approach to interfaith marriage and have created together a relationship that acknowledges the existence of potential problems, while celebrating the love and mutual support of their marriage. They recognize that only through honestly confronting each issue together, as a team, will they continue to resolve important issues, and maintain the loving, successful and satisfying relationship that they have created.

In part due to prior training (Monica is a therapist), and in part because it was a second marriage for both of them, they were very cautious, slow to make important decisions, and as thorough as they could be in their approach to resolving potential interfaith problems in advance.

They both looked into each other's religion, spoke with clergy from the two faiths (Jewish and Catholic), explored the ramifications of an interfaith life for their children, and are an excellent role model for any couple who takes this challenge seriously.

"We discovered that the most important aspect of our marriage is simply *communication,*" Monica admitted when asked how they avoided conflict with each other. "Open and honest communication has been the savior—no pun intended—of our relationship.

"I went to a rabbi before we got married, without Bill. I wanted to discuss books to read, possible problems that he would anticipate, the issue of conversion, and the acceptance of our children in the Jewish community if their mother was Catholic.

"It made our life much easier to learn that in Reform and Reconstructionist Judaism a child is considered Jewish if either parent is Jewish and the child is raised as a Jew, whether or not the other parent formally converts to Judaism.

"Reading and discussing with each other some of the books on religion that the rabbi suggested also brought us closer together. One rule that I suggest to others is, *Don't listen to friends and family who know less than you do about it.*"

"Yes," Bill interjected, "they are all filled with 'good' advice, but they really mostly have no experience with this type of situation at all. In all honesty, they don't have any idea what they are talking about so their advice ought to be taken with a large grain of salt. It's just that everyone feels somehow compelled to say something anyway."

Bill and Monica created a way of approaching their marriage that was thoughtful and serious, and which expressed a willingness to look honestly and directly at the implications of the relationship they had chosen to develop together. They are excellent models for others because of the care that they took to confront directly the issues and questions that many think about, but hesitate to bring into the open.

It has undoubtedly been said by countless marriage counselors that marriage doesn't make problems go away; at best, it simply postpones them. No one helps a relationship or a marriage by trying to prevent conflict through avoidance of important issues and much-needed discussions.

Your feelings should be prized among your most precious and important possessions. They need care and feeding in as many ways as possible throughout every relationship you choose to create. Denying them, ignoring them, or trying to wish them away will only sow the seeds of resentment and anger, which will in turn inevitably be directed toward the one you love and become a source of dissension and disillusionment later.

There are times, of course, when it helps to have a sympathetic shoulder to cry on. More importantly, it is often very helpful to have someone, or several people whom you trust, with whom you can discuss your concerns, questions, anxieties, and doubts.

At times that person will be your local clergy person—a rabbi, minister, or priest with whom you have a good relationship. I have found that, as a whole, clergy are very open to providing a healthy sounding board for your questions, and in general do their best to be nonjudgmental and not overly prejudiced toward one particular religiously "correct" decision.

If you don't feel comfortable going to a member of the clergy, a therapist or counselor can often be very helpful in guiding you through a process of values clarification and discovery.

For many, neither a clergy person nor a therapist is necessary. All that they really need is the willing ear of a loving family member or friend. After all, that's what family and friends are all about—being there in your times of stress and important decision-making. Use your family, and use your friends. Try out your ideas, arguments, fears, what-if's, shouldn't-I's, and what-do-you-think-about's on the people with whom you are closest. They will see it as a compliment to them, a sign of your trust and respect for them, and they inevitably rise to the occasion with sensitivity and caring.

The focus of this entire chapter has really been on the importance of taking control of your life, your decisions, and your relationships. It is up to you to decide exactly how your life will turn out. Since no one can make decisions for you, and ultimately no one else has to live with the decisions that you make for yourself, be courageous enough to do exactly what your inner self *knows* is right for you.

Listen to the still, small voice within you, for it usually is whispering the truth. If you are only willing to listen to that inner voice, you can save yourself years of grief, pain, and heartache.

Trusting yourself is often the hardest task in life. Most couples whose marriages fall apart will admit under serious questioning that in their hearts they knew all along that the relationship was wrong for them. They knew it, but were seduced into discounting their own true feelings, intuitions, and good judgment by the lure of their idealized picture of marriage, of finally experiencing what it was like to be on their own as self-sufficient adults.

Don't allow yourself to fall into this trap. Let your feelings be your guide, not your childhood fantasies or the social pressures that constantly pull at you.

Interfaith marriages need an even stronger foundation upon which to build and grow than same-faith marriages. Give yourself the gift of time, of breathing space to truly discover the reasons for your desire to get married to this specific person at this specific time in your life. This is the most important form of preventive medicine against divorce that I know of. Sometimes it involves being willing to suffer the temporary pain of letting go of relationships that do not fulfill these fundamental criteria for a life of joy and satisfaction.

True, sometimes this medicine is bitter to swallow. Sometimes it does seem easier to close your eyes and shut your ears to the persistent sounds of your own inner protest. Yet, life becomes filled with meaning and fulfillment only when we are courageous enough to choose what is truly right for us over what is merely expedient.

Marriage is one of the most beautiful inventions of the human spirit. It is an opportunity for one unique personality to embrace the soul of another, joining mind, body, and spirit to create yet a third distinct entity called us.

It is this third entity, which we call the relationship, that will become a thing of joy and delight only to the extent that the two who create it fit one with the other.

Say "I do" to the question: "Do you want your life to be filled with excitement, purpose, and love?" Say "I do" to the responsibility to choose thoughtfully and carefully, with the commitment to be honest with yourself. Make sure that you don't say "I do" to marriage until you have discovered a relationship that you know will provide you with all the love that you truly deserve. Then you can move on to creating the rest of your life as a team, together.

THE
INTERFAITH
WEDDING

Chapter V

How to Tell Your Parents "We're Getting Married!"

"My mom wanted me to marry someone from her religion. She's very religious and was upset about the possibility that I might marry Aron. What could I do? I fell in love with him, and that was that."

—Deidre, twenty-one, interfaith married for one year

When Dan and Brenda first came to see me, they had already decided to get married. Dan, twenty-nine and Jewish, and Brenda, twenty-seven and Catholic, had known each other for seventeen years. They grew up in the same neighborhood, went to the same schools, enjoyed the same life-style, and fell in love with each other along the way.

Both of them were concerned with how their parents would take the news of their decision. "Part of the reason that we have waited for several years to make any decision at all is because of what we fear our parents will say," Dan said. "They have known each other for a long time, too, but none of them will be particularly thrilled to learn that Brenda and I have finally decided to get married."

"I'm really worried about how my parents will react," Brenda added. "They like Dan of course; he's practically part of the family by now anyway. But it's the fine line between 'practically' and 'definitely' that makes the difference. My parents are church-going Catholics, and they are not going to be happy at the prospect of their grandchildren slipping away into Judaism."

"If you think *they* will be upset," Dan interjected, "wait until you hear *my* parents. The very thought of my children not having a Bar or Bat Mitzvah, let alone becoming Catholics in any way, will be enough to send them to the moon without a rocket. Frankly, Rabbi, although we love each other a lot and are sure that our relationship will work out, we are both scared to just walk up to our parents and say, 'Hi, Mom and Dad, guess what. We've decided to get married.' Help!"

Dan and Brenda are typical of many interfaith couples who experience fear and trepidation at the prospect of confronting their parents with the news. In this chapter we will learn how some couples have successfully coped with the problem.

As with most aspects of interfaith relationships, the important principle is to communicate in such a way that it doesn't become a win/lose situation. There is absolutely no reason why *everyone* cannot be a winner, as long as you define "winning" as leaving each person with their dignity and sense of self-esteem intact.

Dan and Brenda's overriding consideration was how to tell their parents in a way that demonstrated a sensitivity to *their* feelings. Obviously, each situation requires its own form of tact and diplomacy. The same message can be communicated two different ways and achieve totally different results. There is an ancient Arab legend that captures this perfectly:

> Once there was a king who called upon his two soothsayers and prophets to foretell the future. The first came to the king and said, "Your Majesty, as I look into the future I see a great personal disaster for you and your family. Your two sons will both die before you." The king was outraged at this prophecy and immediately commanded that the insolent soothsayer's head be cut off. Then he called for the second prophet. This time, the wise soothsayer bowed low before the king and said, "Your Royal Highness, I see for you a long and prosperous life. In fact, you are so healthy and virile that you will outlive your entire family." The king was so pleased by this wonderful report that he ordered the prophet rewarded with bags of gold and silver. The moral of the story? It's not the message, it's how you communicate it that counts.

Being sensitive to parents' feelings does not mean suppressing your own needs and desires. It simply means going out of your way to show them that you care about them enough to take their feelings into consideration. For most parents, that demonstration alone will sufficiently soften the blow of the announcement so that a reasonably supportive reaction will occur.

Brenda told me, "My biggest concern was the feelings of my in-laws-to-be. I knew that Dan and I would be fine regardless of the type of ceremony that we had, but we knew that having a rabbi marry us was really important to his mom. When we talked it over, Dan and I decided that if it was important to her, we'd make it important to us, too."

There are those who see this reaction as somehow hypocritical, saying, "It's a mockery of someone's deep religious feelings to ask a rabbi or a priest to officiate at your ceremony simply to make your parents happy." I disagree. The sixth commandment has been "Honor your father and mother" for several thousand years, and I can think of no more concrete demonstration of that honor and respect than to allow their deeply held religious beliefs to influence and shape the very nature of *your* wedding. To me that is a beautiful wedding gift, from you to them, and something of which you can be proud.

The problem arises when your parents are less than open and above board with you about how they really feel. Brenda went on to comment, "My mom said it was fine with her if we had a Jewish ceremony, but I guess she wasn't really honest with us about her feelings. She became unhappy with it as the wedding itself drew near, but never came out and told us. I guess she wanted a Catholic wedding after all, although that would have been impossible since Dan is Jewish. I think the real problem was that she felt left out, and if I'd known that, we would have figured out a way to make her feel more included."

This is a good lesson for everyone. It isn't any easier for parents to be honest and open with you about their feelings than it is for you to be totally honest about yours to them. Sometimes it takes a little probing, a little prodding, some help from another family member, relative, or close friend, to uncover their true desires. Most couples if properly informed can find some way to make their parents happier with the situation, if they only know that the problem exists in the first place.

Among other things, going out of your way to discover your parents' true feelings tells them "This marriage to someone of another religious background is *not* a rejection of you or my family. I still love you and want you to be happy too."

Jack, twenty-five, who had no religious background at all, and Diane, twenty-three and Jewish, found themselves on the tail end of a spiral with his parents over pre-wedding plans. In fact, Jack told me, "We tried to shelter them because we thought that would be in their best interest, and then they felt left out and it backfired. It got so complicated that it just seemed like we couldn't do anything right."

"The main problem was simply that we didn't know how to ask his parents what *they* wanted to do about some of the wedding plans," Diane added, "so we made decisions on their behalf, and that got us deeper and deeper in trouble."

It should be obvious just from these two examples that feeling "left out" is one of the most prevalent parental problems when it comes to interfaith marriages. At times it seems as if *everyone* feels left out, no matter who they are, or what decisions are being made. The best strategy is always the most direct. *Ask them what they want.*

Should We Tell Them Together Or Alone?

When it comes to certain decisions, there is no right answer. You simply have to use your best judgment given the personalities of your parents, your individual relationships with them, the length of time you have been together, and *your* relative comfort in the situation.

Tell them alone, if you think the situation needs more smoothing over, more warm-up, more parent-to-child relationship building. Tell them together, if your relationship has been a long-term one, or you both already have good "in-law" relationships, or you simply want to present a united front as secure, loving partners.

The key to success is to go with your instincts and feelings. You both probably know your own parents well enough, and even each other's parents well enough, to decide if it is more comfortable for you to make the announcement alone or together.

Parents are people too and have their own range of unpredictable feelings when it comes to the lives of their children. There are times, and there are parent/child relationships, that truly demand outside intervention to keep the peace. If there is a trusted friend, a respected family member, sibling, or even outside clergy person you can call upon to help with their adjustment to the reality of your relationship, don't hesitate to utilize them. Remember, at all times the goal is to maintain the best possible relationship with all the parents so that you won't have to first overcome negative comments, actions, and feelings before you can establish a supportive and sympathetic relationship with them *after* the wedding takes place.

Jack and Diane eventually worked their way out of their parental problem with the help of two of Diane's relatives. "My grandma and aunt, who are really religious, were behind what we were doing. They managed to smooth things over for the rest of the family, including my parents. After all, who could argue with Granny! Since Grandma liked Jack, everybody else in the family found it easier to accept him and our decision.

If there is a matriarch or patriarch in the family tree, do your best to win them over. They generally have the most influence among the rest of the family, and most of the time their support will help win the acceptance of the rest.

Wanting Parental Approval

For many interfaith couples the rejection of parents and the loss of their approval can be among the most devastating results of their decision to marry. It is difficult, no matter how old we become, whether it is our first, second, or third marriage, to be a child facing the disapproval of our parents.

All of us experience tension in separating from our parents and developing our own individuation as independent adults on the deepest psychological level. All of us continue to long in some way for the security of our parents' emotional embrace.

Parental approval of our mate can be an important psychological acknowledgment of our adult status in the world. It is a way for us to feel that we are recognized as responsible adult members of society by the people whose opinion counts the most—our parents.

In part this accounts for the depth of anguish that often accompanies parental rejection of an intended life partner. At the same time, there are those who marry when they are older and more experienced at dealing with life's disappointments and rejections, who find it easier to cope with the lack of support from their parents regarding their marriage plans.

For Bill and Monica, both entering into their second marriage, both mature adults, this was certainly the case. "My family was actually happier that he was Jewish than if he had been Protestant," Monica told me. "They all felt that it would be easier to create a life together with a Jewish man and his family than it would be to reconcile a Catholic and a Protestant religious life.

"Although they weren't particularly thrilled to learn that Bill and I were getting married, by this time in my life (and after a reasonable amount of therapy), I have sufficiently resolved enough parent/child issues that their approval would be nice, but isn't necessary for my peace of mind or happiness."

For most, however, parental approval is still a prize to be sought after. Aron and Deidre described how they had successfully overcome a very strong initial opposition on the part of Deidre's Protestant mother to the fact that Deidre was marrying a Jewish man.

It was Deidre's mother who seemed to put up most of the resistance to the wedding, and it was she who ultimately gave us a clue to one of the most successful strategies available for breaking down barriers between your parents and your mate.

Deidre and Aron live in San Diego, while Deidre's mother lives in New Jersey. For several years their relationship had been primarily conducted through weekly phone calls back and forth. The result was that Deidre's mother had felt out of touch with her daughter's daily life for some time; this contributed to much of the intensity with which she opposed Deidre's engagement and eventual marriage to Aron. Not only did she express a natural parental concern for her child and the adult decisions that she was making so far away across the country, but since she lived 3,000 miles away she also didn't know Aron from Adam.

Every person wants to know, and on some level give their approval, to the choice of a lifetime mate for their child. They'd really like the child to *ask* permission, but of course in this day and age that is becoming rarer and rarer. Deidre's mother was experiencing the frustration of not knowing her daughter's intended life partner *at all*. Under the circumstances, her strong negative reaction was hardly a surprise.

The solution to Deidre's problem with her mother was much simpler than it initially appeared. First, Aron and Deidre flew her mother out to San Diego from New Jersey for a visit. This gave them all a chance to get to know each other and for Deidre to spend some mother/daughter time alone with her.

This time alone proved to be very important to both of them, for it allowed them to openly discuss their feelings with each other face to face. It also allowed them to reinforce their relationship and love for each other, and to allow Deidre's mother to reestablish her sense of connection with her daughter's life.

In addition to the positive benefits for the mother/daughter relationship, it also gave Aron and Deidre's mother a chance to spend some time together so she could transcend the impersonal label the-Jewish-man-who-wants-to-marry-my-daughter, and begin to see him as an individual. She could now experience him as simply a loving, caring, giving, sensitive, mature man who happened to be both Jewish and in love with her daughter.

Deidre said, "My mom wanted me to marry in her religion. She's very religious and was upset about my marriage plans. What could I do? I fell in love with someone who was both older *and* Jewish. Now that she knows Aron, she loves him and neither age nor religion is a factor anymore.

"I think that this is the key to many potential problems within the family—getting to know each other as people, beyond the labels of Jew or Christian. That is the only way to break down the barriers that exist as a result of stereotypes, prejudices, and fears of the unknown 'other.' It certainly worked for us."

The parental approval issue is also connected to the difficulty some participants in interfaith relationships have in integrating into their partner's larger family structure. When Heather, a born-again Christian, got engaged to Eddie, who was Jewish, this problem seemed almost insurmountable.

"I was a bit overwhelmed by his family at first," Heather said. "They seemed so overbearing, so totally involved in Eddie's life. I guess I just never had any experience of your typical 'Jewish mother' before, and I wasn't sure how I was supposed to handle it. I knew immediately that they would want to be totally involved in our wedding plans, and that the chances were I would have to fight for every bit of control that I could get over my own wedding.

"We lived together before we got married, and I think that really helped us. First of all it brought us closer together as a team, knowing that we could live successfully as a couple. Second, it gave me the chance to see what Eddie's family was like.

"I was able to attend their holiday celebrations and get a sense of what it would be like to be a part of their family in advance. Of course, it also gave his family a chance to get to know me before the wedding, which I think is crucial in order to have a smooth transition into someone else's family, particularly if they are of a different religion.

"When my father heard that I wasn't getting married by a minister in his church, he got really upset. The funny part is that a year or so later, *he* married a Jew too! It helps to remember that you really never know what will change, and how things will suddenly turn around for you tomorrow.

"It was a bit hard for him at first to adjust to the idea of a synagogue wedding. First he heard it was in a temple, and *then* he heard by a rabbi, and *then* he heard there would be some Hebrew in it, too.

"This was one of those circumstances when I just had to say, 'It's my life and it's my marriage. It's my husband and you just have to accept my own choices as an adult.' I told him I was sorry it wasn't what he wanted, but that I couldn't deny myself and my own feelings just to please him. Of course it bothered me that I was disappointing my dad, but the wedding was for *me,* and what he wanted for me wasn't what I wanted for myself."

Eddie had been sitting quietly and nodding his head throughout

Heather's discourse. Finally he added, "In the long run her father really gained respect for her because she stood up for what she believed in, was honest with her feelings, never made it seem like she was 'rejecting' her family. She simply was choosing to marry the man she loved, who happened to be Jewish, and for whom a Jewish ceremony was very important. I must admit that I was very proud of how she handled the whole thing, and not so sure that if the shoe were on the other foot I would be able to do as well."

Lee and Judy, who had been married for fifteen years at the time of our interview, also had developed an attitude that made it easier for them to make their own decisions about their interfaith relationship without either parental approval or guilt.

"My parents hoped that our kids would be raised Catholic," Lee said. "I thought that my mother would be very unhappy with my choice of a Jewish marriage partner, but we just got married anyway. I didn't even discuss it with them first. I felt that I was an adult who could make his own decisions, and by the time they got involved it was a *fait accompli.*

"I decided the best way to avoid conflict was to take total control of the situation, so I took Judy to Las Vegas and we eloped. By the time we came back we were married, and there wasn't much they could do to intervene."

"We decided that we had to live for ourselves first and not for our parents or their expectations of us," Judy added. "You really can't live with yourself if you live that way. You can't spend your life trying to please your parents. The truth is you can't always please them anyway, so you are better off simply taking care of yourself, living the best life that you can, and taking whatever comes as a result."

The Latent Parenting Syndrome

Judy has just touched on one of the most helpful suggestions anyone could possibly give—take care of yourself and your needs first, and *then* do your best to make your parents happy, too. One of the reasons that this is so important to your own mental health and the health of your relationship is that when it comes to interfaith relationships, parents have an uncanny habit of acting unpredictably and out of character.

One of the most confusing aspects of interfaith marriage for those who excitedly announce their impending wedding to less-than-eager-parents and family members is the *intensity* of parental disapproval that they encounter. What perplexes interfaith couples the most is that very often the same parents that they have always perceived to be "not very religious" suddenly emerge as passionate defenders of the faith, whether that faith be Catholic, Protestant, or Jewish.

For example, when John and Melony announced their engagement, both sets of parents immediately began pressuring their respective children to rethink their decision. At the time they shared these reminiscences with me, they had been happily married for over sixteen years.

Even after all these years, they both vividly remembered the days prior to their wedding. Melony told me, "The thing that upset me the most about their reaction was their inability to articulate exactly *why* they were against it. They had never been particularly Jewish, never went to temple, never belonged to Jewish organizations, and yet when I announced my engagement to John, both my parents all of a sudden emerged as kind of 'closet Jews.' They kept saying how very strongly they felt about the whole religion issue, and things like 'How could you do this to us?' It just seemed crazy to me since they didn't lead a very good Jewish life."

John continued, "In the end we had a beautiful Jewish ceremony. I knew that Melony's parents weren't happy about the whole thing, but they really never said why, except once when they told her 'What will we tell the relatives?' which made us both think that they were mostly just embarrassed at what they imagined their more observant Jewish relatives would think about them as parents. I really think that they felt guilty somehow, like they had failed as parents or something."

Melony added, "I fought a lot with them. They said that they wouldn't invite the relatives to a service without a rabbi. They really wanted John to convert to Judaism, but I didn't think that was fair to him, and it wasn't important to me. When we agreed to a Jewish ceremony, that naturally helped a lot."

"It was my choice to do what my wife wanted to do," John stated. "It seems to me my upbringing in Minnesota was without Jews altogether, so I never had any bias one way or the other about them."

Melony and John encountered what I call the latent parenting syndrome. This refers to the discovery on the part of parents who have previously been uninvolved with religion of a religious awakening, which amazingly seems to coincide with the very moment they learn of an impending marriage between their child and someone of another faith. It often is difficult for the couple to handle, particularly because nine times out of ten they are taken totally by surprise and are consequently quite unprepared to respond to this sudden rush of religious fervor.

The main problem that seems to arise as a result of this syndrome is that it throws up an instant barrier to understanding, and unless the parents and children are able to break through these communication barriers to reconnect with the love and caring that truly does exist between them, they are often driven farther and farther apart.

In thinking back over this particularly difficult period in their relationship, John recalled, "We finally decided that if we couldn't find a rabbi who would marry us, or if having a rabbi didn't satisfy Melony's parents, we would just run away and get married alone somewhere."

"It was really terrible for a while," Melony added. "I felt like our wedding was for others more than it was for us, and that made me unhappy and angry. It's not a very wonderful way to begin your married life together!"

"Her mother even told me once, 'Unless you convert I won't have anything to do with you,'" John added. "In a sense it seemed like they were only concerned with *their* feelings and not *ours,* or even their own daughter's. After the rabbi decision, things definitely got better with them. Sometimes things seem funny, like when my mother said she didn't have a problem with the fact that Melony was Jewish, it was just that she wasn't good enough for her son."

Both John and Melony eventually realized (with a little help from the rabbi who married them) that Melony's parents were reacting in a way that revealed a tremendous amount of guilt over their *own* lack of involvement in their religion. It is a fairly common experience for parents to see their own religious identity as independent of any specific religious observance that they may or may not have incorporated into their daily lives in the past.

This is particularly evident within the Jewish community. Judaism is more than a religion; it is a religious civilization that includes ritual, culture, language, emotional attachment to the land of Israel, religion, and above all a sense of peoplehood and connection to the Jewish community that for many *is* their primary form of Jewish identification.

The latent parenting syndrome is particularly prevalent among Jewish parents, since they may identify very strongly with their connection to the Jewish *people,* while not feeling a particular need to express their Judaism in any particular *religious* observance.

The problem is that this becomes very confusing to their children, who may see only the surface lack of religious observance and grow up with the impression that their parents are "not very religious" at all.

I have found that often it is the parents themselves who are unaware of their own feelings until a child's wedding announcement suddenly turns on their religious identity switch. The reaction that has just been described is often a complex interaction between unexpressed religious identity and guilt over an apparent lack of adequate parenting skills. It is quite common for parents of interfaith couples to feel guilty over the way they have raised their children; it is seen as a sense of personal parental failure to have their children choose what appears to be a significantly different life-style and perhaps even a different value system. The most successful strategy is also the simplest—confront these issues head on.

Diane and Jack are typical of how this problem can be resolved through direct supportive confrontation. In this case, it was Jack's mother who suddenly "got religion" the minute the wedding plans were announced.

"It wasn't really until we decided to be married by a rabbi that his mother got upset," Diane said. "It surprised us both, since Jack hadn't been raised in any particular religion at all, and when I had asked him what he was, he couldn't even say for sure."

"Yes," Jack responded, shaking his head as he recalled how surprised they were at the time, "I couldn't believe that she reacted so strongly to the thought of a Jewish wedding. I never went to any church, I couldn't tell you what religion my mom or dad were, and here all of a sudden 'Christianity' becomes a big, important thing to her.

"At first, I just couldn't figure the whole thing out at all. After I calmed down from the initial surprise, Diane and I began to explore together what we thought was really going on. I don't know how we arrived at this particular strategy, but when we did we both instantly felt better, even before we had confronted my mom.

"What we did was really quite simple. I went to my mom in private, since we felt that would make it easier for her to open up, and she wouldn't feel like there were two against one and that it was some kind of emotional battle going on.

"All I did was say what I thought was going on in her mind. I said something like, 'If I were in your place I imagine that I would probably feel exactly the same way you do, and probably I'd even feel a little scared that my son was about to move away from me into a totally different and foreign life-style and world. That would definitely scare me, too.'

"My mom admitted that she did have those feelings, and that she felt like she had failed me as a mother in some way. Then I had the chance to hug and kiss her and tell her that I didn't think she had failed, that I loved her and thought she was the best mother in the world and really appreciated how much she was worried about me.

"She felt a lot better after we had spoken, particularly because I assured her that marrying someone Jewish was not a rejection of her or the kind of person that she wanted me to be. I told her that I was marrying Diane because I loved her and wanted to share my life with her, not because I was rejecting or running away from my family. By the time I was through she didn't really care what kind of wedding we had, since she felt she wasn't losing me to some other life after all."

After dealing with hundreds of interfaith couples over the years, it is clear to me that probably the most important strategy for maintaining a positive, loving relationship with your parents is to very clearly communicate to them that marrying someone of a different religion *is not a rejection of them or their values*. In fact, most of the time, it actually turns out to be a *validation* of the values that they have instilled in you since early childhood.

Most parents of interfaith couples, when asked whether or not *they* taught values to their children that allowed them to feel comfortable marrying someone of a different religion, admit that it is true. Most parents of interfaith couples realize that they taught their children tolerance and respect for all people, that all people are worthwhile, are worthy of dignity and ultimately embrace the same human values of peace, love, justice, compassion, and striving for a better world for all.

It is often helpful when interfaith couples point this out to their parents. Reminding them that you took their teachings seriously, and you have discovered that, at least when it comes to your mate, everything that they taught you is true, often helps pave the way for more understanding and tolerance within the family.

Let your parents know that *your love for them has not changed*. Tell them that your values have not changed, that your membership within the family and all it represents is still very important to you.

Feelings of parental failure are among the most universal results of interfaith marriages. When left unacknowledged and unaddressed, these feelings of failure are often the hidden source of a tremendous amount of tension and stress between parents and their children. Listen to some parents themselves, as they share *their* side of the story, and you will see just how typical these feelings really are.

Eleanor, a 63-year-old Jewish mother whose daughter has been married to a Catholic man seventeen years, shared her own feelings with me.

"At first I was devastated. I couldn't believe *my* daughter would do such a thing to me. That's just how I saw it at the time; as if she were doing something to *me*. My husband and I literally shouted our disapproval, ranting and raving about the big mistake she was making, and our feelings of shame in the community.

"We really gave them both such a bad time about it that it left tension and strong resentments between us still for all these years.

Her husband basically has never forgiven us for putting them through the emotional turmoil that we created.

"We both felt such tremendous feelings of failure as parents that we asked each other over and over again, 'Where did we go wrong? What could we have done differently?'

"Eventually we realized that it really wasn't anything we had done or not done at all, and that our daughter is her own person with her own values and her own life to live. If we had it to do over, I know we would react very differently. I advise all my friends who have children who intermarry, 'Don't reject them, don't shove them away from you; it will only hurt you and your relationship in the end.'"

Ernestine, whose son also married a woman of another faith, said, "I told myself, 'Either you accept this girl or you'll lose your son.' That's really the crux of the issue. Besides, other than the fact that she's a different religion, I love everything about her.

"My own parents, who would have killed *me* if I'd intermarried, came to me when my son did and said, 'What can you do, cut off your nose to spite your face?' I have always tried to support my son through life, and I want him to feel that I am still there for him if and when he needs me."

I constantly receive phone calls and visits from parents who are seeking advice as to how to handle the recent news of a child's impending marriage to someone of another religion.

Each time I ask these parents, knowing that they are truly suffering emotional pain, "Would you rather be right or happy? Being 'right' allows you to vent your frustrations toward your child, act out of a sense of self-righteousness, and invariably alienate yourself from the child that you truly love.

"Choosing the 'happy' alternative, although it doesn't give you everything you want—but how many parents get everything they want from their children under *any* circumstances?—does allow you to maintain an open, supportive, loving relationship with your child, which to my mind is the preferable outcome."

Carolyn's daughter married a man of a different religion fifteen years ago. Unlike Eleanor, Carolyn had the presence of mind to think through the implications of her reactions before she stridently announced her disapproval.

"We thought it over and decided that if we were to object

strongly to the marriage, it would only alienate us from our kids. My husband was from the old school and was not happy at all, but I told him if we created a lot of upset and tension, we just would never see them at all."

My own experience interviewing and counseling interfaith couples has demonstrated very clearly to me that strong parental objections are taken most often as a challenge to the couple's love for each other.

The natural human reaction is for the couple to bond even closer together, strengthen their resolve to make their own decisions as adults in their own way, and if anything to get married even more quickly than they otherwise might have.

I have often found, particularly with interfaith relationships, that more important than *what* you say is *how* you say it. The following scenario, for example, is unfortunately one of the most common results of what I refer to as "unassertive interfaith communication" between parents, in-laws, and the couple about to be married.

Joyce is about to get married to the man of her dreams, and her girlfriend Cookie has been holding her hand through the entire process. From what I know of interfaith marriages, the conversation might sound something like this:

JOYCE: "I can't believe it. I'm getting married in *one week.* There are still so many things to do that I feel like the proverbial chicken with my head cut off!"

COOKIE: "Calm down, Joyce, take it easy. Everything will be just fine. I promise you'll have the perfect wedding."

JOYCE: "I know I shouldn't be worrying so much, but there are so many things that can go wrong, so many details to take care of, so many relatives throwing their two cents in, telling me the 'right' way to do everything, which is of course *their* way . . . I don't know if I'll make it through all this pressure."

COOKIE: "What pressure? I thought you and Marty already made all the arrangements for everything, so what's to worry about?"

JOYCE: "Well, for starters, even after we agreed on the kind of ceremony we would have, found a beautiful hotel in which to have it, and a wonderful Unitarian minister to perform a nonsectarian ceremony, his *mother* is constantly giving us 'advice.' She acts as if, even at this late date, we still might change the ceremony to her temple, or 'at least' find a rabbi to do the wedding, 'if you really care about my feelings . . .'

"I can't tell you how ticked off I get every time she starts up about it. Then *I* say something in return, and Marty starts defending his mother, and he and I get in an argument, and I end up in tears or he ends up slamming doors. It's driving me crazy.

"Oh, yes, of course there is the possibility that in the end his mother might not even show up at the ceremony at all. She might just be too 'uncomfortable' with the whole thing. Believe me, it wouldn't bother *me* at all. In fact, I probably would be relieved, but Marty would be upset, and it would put a damper on the whole thing. Why can't she just be happy that I love her son as much as I do and stay out of it?"

Cookie, having heard this over and over again for months, does her best to be sympathetic. In the end, however, she can only respond weakly, "Well, look on the bright side—it will all be over after next week and you can get on with your life together and forget all about these hassles."

The sad reality is that for all too many couples the end of the wedding doesn't mark the end of their in-law and parent problems. For many, it is simply a foretaste of the bittersweet in-law relationships that plague so many interfaith marriages. For some, the problems that begin with the wedding continue throughout their relationship, causing strife among the couple themselves and seriously contributing to the eventual collapse of their marriage.

Such difficulties are *not*, however, inevitable. With the proper planning, cooperation, and assertive communication, every couple has the chance to weather parent/in-law storms successfully and emerge into the calm and peaceful waters of marital harmony and love.

An Assertive Child/Parent
Communication Model

Let's look at some specific strategies for coping with potential in-law/parent stress. The fundamental idea is for you to *take control* of the situation in a calm, supportive, yet assertive (*not* aggressive) manner.

For example, if a problem arises about some aspect of the wedding with which your future in-laws aren't happy, try a bold and direct approach. Take them out to lunch!

Sit down and say, "I love your son/daughter very much, and we both have made a decision that I understand you are not happy with. My relationship with you is very important to me, and I want you to be happy, too. I would very much like to establish a relationship with you based on honest and straightforward communication. Whether or not we agree on everything is secondary to our ability to keep an open line of communication between us.

"We obviously disagree about certain things in our wedding, and I feel badly about that. I wish I could magically please everyone who is important to John/Mary and me, but it seems that no matter what I do, somebody is unhappy with the decision. I suppose that is just the way things are when so many people are involved.

"I guess John/Mary and I are ultimately going to have to make our own decisions and hope that the people who love us will support us, even if they might have done it differently. We are counting on the love of our families to help us get through this high-pressure time, and along with suggestions and advice, we need your love and support. Can we count on you?"

Now I guarantee that *nobody* has ever talked to your prospective in-laws, or your own parents for that matter, like that.

This technique allows others to express their feelings to you, gets the issues out in the open where they belong, and puts in proper perspective that the wedding you are planning together is based on two people in love, committed to each other, who are planning on sharing their lives together. The ceremony itself is presented as an expression of the two of you and your love, and as such *you* must be responsible for the ultimate decisions that are made.

The technique known as negative assertion often comes in very handy when dealing with parents and in-laws. For example, you might say to them: "I really feel foolish about this, and I know you must think I'm such a flake for changing my mind, but I'd really like to have my cousins as flower girl and ring bearer instead of the people we originally said. I really feel silly and know that you must think I'm crazy for changing my mind all the time."

To your surprise, you may hear your parents/in-laws say: "Oh, of course it's okay to change your mind. There's nothing flaky or silly about it at all, dear. You're planning your wedding, and you're under lots of stress every minute to make a million different decisions. It's perfectly natural to have second thoughts about things. Etc., etc."

The natural tendency of human beings is to defend people who cast themselves in an underdog role, who express out loud their own perceived inadequacies and failures. That gives your parents/in-laws an opportunity to be magnanimous and caring and to rise above petty concerns, and most of the time that is exactly what happens. I suggest you take a class in assertiveness training, or read a book on the subject (there are several good ones available at your local bookstore), as it will help you tremendously in dealing with this high-pressure time in your life.

Many couples find themselves bending over backward in an attempt not to hurt their parents' feelings, yet discover that in trying so hard to avoid conflict, they have simply exacerbated the problem. This happens most often over issues that relate to spending money on the upcoming wedding.

"The rehearsal dinner was a big area of tension for us," Diane said. "We didn't know if Jack's parents would be comfortable hosting it or not, and we weren't sure how to go about approaching the subject sensitively, especially since we knew they were aware that my parents had more money than they did and were spending a lot on the wedding. Jack found an article on what grooms' parents do and left it for them to read as one feeble way of dealing with the problem."

"We tried to shelter them," Jack interjected, "but it backfired.

They ended up feeling left out, and had their feelings hurt because they thought we didn't *care* if they were involved or not."

"There is a good lesson here for interfaith couples," Diane added. "We didn't know how to ask his parents what *they* wanted to do. There was tension over where to have the dinner, and the best thing to have done would simply have been to sit down with them and talk it all out.

"If we had only shared *our* feelings openly and honestly, we could have told them that we were uncomfortable because we loved them and didn't want them to feel bad. Then they could have told us that they felt fine simply being as much a part of our wedding as they could. As it was, every decision turned into a major area of conflict, hurt feelings, and upset.

"Since Jack couldn't handle his mom's upset, and the tension that we kept creating by not communicating, he stopped calling her. Now we realize that was a mistake, and if we had it to do over again, we would both call more, talk more, talk things out to clear the air, and make *sure* that we forced each other to communicate on issues that are important."

Taking control of your wedding is probably the single most difficult task in the entire process, from the moment of announcement to the moment of the ceremony itself. Doing whatever you need to do to insure that the wedding is what *you* want it to be is probably the best gift you can give to each other, and will be an important statement to yourselves and your families about the nature of your relationship.

"I think the best way to do it, in retrospect, is to present it to your parents as: 'This is what *we* want, this is what *we* decided. We are delighted to listen to all the advice and suggestions that the family has to offer, but ultimately it is *our* decision about *our* wedding,'" Diane declared. "It would have been nice to be able to have said and done that, but at the time we just weren't emotionally able. Everything seemed so overwhelming."

Remember, if you can't count on each other to be supporting your joint decisions, negotiating with parents on each other's behalf, and standing up for each other's feelings and desires, then your marriage is starting on extremely rocky ground. If so, you'd better step back and look at the kind of relationship you are creating together in the first place.

Ultimately, the process of telling your parents that you are getting married can serve as an important precedent for everyone involved. As you demonstrate to each other and your parents and in-laws that you function as a team, caring for, supporting, and giving emotional nourishment to each other, you will be establishing the kind of pattern for your behavior, and that of your parents as well, that will be an important part of the lifetime fabric of your relationship.

Chapter VI

PLANNING THE WEDDING

"I felt like our wedding was for others more than it was for us."

—Melony, thirty-six, interfaith married sixteen years

As they sat across from my desk one Sunday afternoon, neither Neil nor Sharon were smiling. They had come to discuss their upcoming wedding and had asked me to officiate. Although they were in agreement on many aspects of the ceremony, and in general seemed to be able to discuss most issues dispassionately, all of a sudden they had reached an impasse.

The issue at hand was whether or not a glass would be broken at the end of the ceremony, which is the traditional conclusion to a Jewish wedding. Usually the groom steps on a glass wrapped in a cloth napkin, and Neil was adamantly stating his objections to Sharon in what was rapidly becoming a heated and angry exchange.

This seemingly simple issue can serve as a perfect example of potential conflict resolution in the midst of the tense, emotion-charged environment that often develops as you undertake the delicate task of negotiating the specifics of planning an interfaith wedding.

Sharon couldn't understand Neil's objection to participating in what she thought was a lovely Jewish custom, and Neil, who is not Jewish, felt strongly that he would be uncomfortable doing it. When Sharon asked for an explanation of exactly what Neil's objection was, he finally said that he didn't agree with what he understood the symbolism of the glass to be.

It seems that he had been told that the breaking of the glass was to remind the Jewish people that even in a time of joy they are supposed to remember that the Holy Temple in Jerusalem was destroyed, and they are still waiting for it to be rebuilt, and for God's kingdom to be established on earth. Not only was this not something that he believed in, but he felt that his wedding was a time to be joyous and not remind people of sad things, whatever they may be.

Sharon said she didn't care what the symbolism was about, you just "couldn't have a Jewish wedding without breaking the glass at the end." She had always looked forward to it as a beautiful part of *her* wedding and was very upset that Neil was refusing to do it. Neil was just as adamant about his refusal and kept stressing the fact that he felt the sadness of the symbolism was simply not appropriate for *his* wedding.

In the course of the conversation, Sharon was willing to admit that she too wasn't thrilled with that particular explanation as to why the glass is broken, but all the same she just couldn't imagine getting married without it.

There are a number of different ways that couples can potentially approach problems and conflicts such as the one Sharon and Neil were facing. One approach was for me to present them with an alternative explanation and justification for this particular ritual.

I told them that there are in fact many different interpretations given as to why a glass is broken. Religious symbols are living aspects of a faith community's life, and their origins are often found in the obscurity of the distant past. Often the original meaning of a religious ritual or symbol has been transformed over time from a primitive superstitious beginning to a lofty ethical principle. In each generation, new layers of meaning are added that correspond to the specific cultural realities of that particular age.

When a couple understand this simple fact of the evolving character of religious life, it is easier to discover *with them* a specific meaning or significance for a given religious symbol that they find compatible with their own values and life-style.

In the case of the broken glass at the end of a Jewish wedding, I shared one explanation which they both found to be a positive and even welcome symbol to incorporate into their lives: Often in life there are external circumstances, experiences, events, and influences that seem to impinge upon their relationship. There are even moments when those external influences may look like they are determining the quality of their relationship, yet their potential impact is really as fragile as glass.

Thus, when they break the glass at the end of a wedding ceremony, they are symbolically demonstrating their mastery over all of those outside forces. They are, through that act, acknowledging that it is solely within their hands to make their relationship stronger as the years pass or allow those outside forces to chip away at the integrity of their love and wear it down.

Neil said that with *this* explanation he would be willing to at least consider the idea. I added that given this explanation it seemed most appropriate, if they were to ultimately agree to breaking a glass, that *both* of them should break it. That way, the symbolism would be consistently carried through the ceremony, since it was both of their respective responsibilities to keep the relationship healthy and growing.

After we finished discussing the meaning of the symbol itself, I could see that there was still something bothering Neil, so we continued the discussion at that point on a more personal level, as the crucial step in disagreements such as these is to get underneath the initial responses to the underlying *feelings* that so often go unexpressed.

When a couple argues about a given ritual, symbol, or religious custom, they will often discover something significant underneath all the intellectual "reasons" why they do or do not want to participate in a ritual from another's religious tradition. Through the process of our supportive exploration together, Neil began to realize that his real reason for not wanting to break the glass was a fear of feeling and looking foolish. He realized that it felt inauthentic for him to participate in a "Jewish" ritual when he wasn't Jewish. He was afraid not only of feeling silly, but of making his family uncomfortable as well. As soon as he expressed these feelings, there was at once an easing of tension.

Sharon was relieved that Neil's real reasons had nothing to do with Judaism per se, Jewish rituals, or even the particular meaning of a given religious symbol. In fact, when she realized that his reluctance to break the glass was a result of feelings of fear and embarrassment, she put her arms around him, gave him a hug and told him how much she loved him and didn't ever want him to feel afraid or have his feelings hurt.

They kissed, held each other's hands, and sighed with relief. In just a few minutes of further conversation they easily resolved the matter; Neil was now willing to embrace the glass-breaking as a fitting conclusion and symbol for their marriage.

"You know," he told me, "now I think breaking the glass is a perfect way to remind us both of how crucial it is for us to communicate our true feelings to each other. Doing that is one way of really taking responsibility for the quality of our relationship and for making it work. Here I am already worrying about what others will think, how *they* will see me, and it's impinging on *our* relationship right now, just as you said. In fact, I'd like to break a glass right here in your study!"

Almost no one can resist the honest expression of another's feelings. It is almost paradoxical that the area of our greatest vulnerability, our feelings, turns out in reality to be the safest ground upon which two struggling hearts can meet. I consistently find myself counseling couples, "When in doubt, search for your true feelings, take a deep breath, and share them with your partner. Trust them with your feelings, as you trust them with your love, and your relationship will be richer for it."

Overcoming Childhood Fantasies

There are no secrets to successfully negotiating the numerous potential pitfalls of wedding planning. It really is not that complicated a task; it just seems that way when you are in the midst of it. As with every aspect of your life together, the single most important components of a successful wedding plan are *communication* and *cooperation* between bride and groom. It is very easy for many people to simply say, "Whatever you want," when they *really* want to scream, "I don't want it *that* way, I want it the way I've always dreamed it would be."

It is important to remember that there is nothing wrong with having strong feelings, especially about the manner and style of your own wedding. In our culture most little girls fantasize and dream about their weddings, and often these long-held, deep-seated dreams and expectations collide with the reality of their adult lives. For many, the fantasy they had as a child is still very much a part of their experience, forming the yardstick against which all their real wedding plans are measured.

Often I have sat with young couples in my study, discussing the tension that has arisen over plans for their wedding, only to discover that the bride-to-be has had in her mind all along a clear picture of *exactly* the kind of wedding she wanted, but had never openly acknowledged that to her fiancé.

Perhaps she was aware of their financial limitations and so didn't want to make him feel guilty for not being able to provide her with what she *really* wanted. The groom, of course, wasn't aware of her childhood dreams at all, had been planning the wedding he *thought* she wanted, and couldn't understand why she seemed so "underwhelmed" and blasé about something that was supposed to be wonderful and exciting.

After talking about it openly, and probing for the deeper feelings, they often discovered that the childhood fantasy held its power only as long as it went unexpressed and unacknowledged. Once it was in the open, the bride would often laugh and say, "I can't believe that I have walked around with that four-year-old girl's idea of a wedding all these years. What I really want is something more like what we have planned already, perhaps with a couple of changes."

Then they can deal with the "couple of changes" as adults who are mutually involved in the decision-making process and most often easily come to an amicable agreement.

It's Your Wedding, So Be Happy

Negotiating your way through the tangled web of wedding plans can be a fun, invigorating, relationship-building experience, *if* you approach it with the correct attitude. The attitude that will serve to enhance the quality of your relationship is one that says, "We are in this together. It is our wedding and we are the ones who will be looking back for the rest of our lives, either smiling at how beautiful and special it was, or cringing at the memory of all the decisions we gave over to others, and all the things that happened in our wedding that we regret."

Use the experience of planning your wedding as an opportunity to do things you haven't done before. Use it as a chance to be creative in the way you handle the day-to-day problems and disagreements that arise between you, your family, and your spouse's family.

The most successful wedding strategy is that which will put you *in control* of both the wedding and your life. *That* is really the key—to be in control, to have the peace of mind and sense of security that come from knowing that *you* have designed the wedding you want together, *you* have chosen the tone and style of this special day in your lives, and *you* have decided who will be invited to share it with you and your families.

Don't get me wrong. The picture I am painting of the ideal wedding experience is not an everyday occurrence—but it *is* possible, and you can be one of those who make it a reality.

For many couples the major struggle is in how to keep the balance between their needs and the needs of their extended family.

For example, Richard was thirty-two and Lisa was twenty when they married. Although he had grown up in a traditional Jewish home in New York, Richard had since turned to secular philosophy and embraced what you might call secular American nondenominational Christianity. After his second daughter was born he told me that he would probably be comfortable in any church that would welcome him and his family and provide a warm, supportive, and friendly "religious" framework in which to raise his two children.

At the time of their wedding, Richard and Lisa went to a minister who agreed to marry them in a secular, nondenominational ceremony. "We really wanted someone that we knew to do it, and we had met and liked this minister," Richard told me. "My biggest problem was that my family was pretty religious, and my sister was very involved in Jewish organizational life in New York and had a hard decision whether to come to my wedding or not. She finally decided to come, but my parents didn't come at all.

"I felt bad that they wouldn't share in my joy and my love with me, and I thought that it was pretty stupid and petty of them to risk alienating me and my wife and whatever grandchildren we might create for them, but that's just the way they are."

"We were engaged and lived together for a year before we were married," Lisa added. "We both thought that was a good idea as a way to get to know each other better. We are so perfectly compatible we even finish each other's sentences half the time.

"We chose a place for the wedding with no religious affiliation at all, and ultimately we tried to both make it comfortable for others and not sacrifice what we wanted at the same time. That's really how we do everything."

That is such a good piece of advice that I want to repeat it. *"We tried to both make it comfortable for others and not sacrifice what we wanted at the same time."* It is what is called a workable compromise. Ninety-nine percent of the time someone will feel slighted, someone will feel that the "other side" was given more importance or weight in the decision-making process. Often the best that you can do is to create a workable compromise with all parties directly involved with the wedding, and simply make sure that *you* are satisfied with the end results.

Choosing the Type of Ceremony

Let's take a look at how a number of actual interfaith couples approached *their* weddings. We will hear, in their own words, the decisions they made regarding the ceremony itself, and the specific ways in which each couple handled the built-in stresses and tensions that are part and parcel of nearly all interfaith marriages.

Andy and Michelle were married in Michelle's hometown of Philadelphia. Andy was thirty-one and Michelle was thirty, and they had known each other for about three years prior to the wedding itself.

Andy had been raised in a Congregational church in Baltimore where most of his family still lived. Michelle was from a Reform

Jewish family in Philadelphia and was the first one in her family to "marry out."

At the time of our interview they had been married for six years. Andy told me, "The most difficult issue in our entire life together was the wedding. I guess it was really the *marriage* itself that was difficult for our parents and relatives, but it was the wedding which became the focal point for all their anxieties and frustrations.

"My parents still are church-going people, and although I was involved with a few Jewish girls in college they weren't really prepared for me to *marry* one. It was a bit difficult for them at first to accept my decision, but of course, in the end they had no real choice.

"Deciding on the type of marriage ceremony and how to raise the kids were difficult decisions. We felt that before the wedding we should decide both issues, so I first went to talk to a pastor. He wasn't really much help, since all he said was, 'Either you have a Christian ceremony or a Jewish ceremony or perhaps combine both.' I knew *that* before I went to talk with him, so I went to see a rabbi that Michelle knew and for some reason or other I really liked him. I decided that since I didn't really feel strongly about my Christian upbringing and Michelle had very strong feelings about *her* religion, a Jewish ceremony would make the most sense for us."

Michelle joined in, adding some of her own recollections. "Andy's parents were very cooperative with us all along. All our parents sat in front during the wedding ceremony, and we essentially did it our own way, with a little help from the rabbi. I was adamant about not being married in a church and wanted to do it in my own temple. I really knew what I wanted from the start, but Andy needed to feel comfortable with that decision."

"I was comfortable with it," Andy responded, "and at the same time I was concerned about my parents' feelings. Even though they live in Baltimore and we live in Philadelphia, it isn't that far away, and they are still a part of my life.

"They go to church every Sunday, and it is an integral part of their lives. Naturally, I wanted them to feel as good as they could about their son's wedding. I wanted them to feel comfortable with the ceremony, so we spent some time with the rabbi discussing my parents and their background and beliefs, and he turned out to be very responsive to my needs.

"My parents wanted to feel that I had spent some time thinking about the wedding before I made the decision and didn't just jump into it. They were afraid that I'd simply go along with whatever Michelle wanted, so I really waited for them, so *they* would feel better, which they did."

"Andy's mom really wanted a minister too, but we told her it wasn't allowed, which is what we thought at the time. Andy was concerned about having too much Hebrew in the ceremony, yet having enough so that I and my parents would be comfortable, too."

"We had been together for several years, and since Michelle has always been involved in her family's synagogue, I had gone to services there many times with her and her family. By the time the wedding came, I felt comfortable enough in the synagogue to actually enjoy it, even though I don't know any Hebrew. The services are mostly in English anyway.

"My parents chose not to be very involved with the wedding itself, which probably helped to keep the friction and tension to a minimum. They hosted the rehearsal dinner for us, and that was it. In fact, other than my parents, my brother, and a couple of my parents' closest friends, there were hardly any non-Jews at the ceremony. To tell you the truth, with all our concern for their feelings, after the fact they told me that they enjoyed the ceremony a lot. That made us both feel good."

Andy and Michelle are typical of many interfaith couples. In this case, much of the potential conflict between families was averted by the noninvolvement of the parents whose religious ceremony was not chosen.

Anne and David demonstrate yet another model of how an interfaith couple worked out potential conflicts over their wedding by the willingness of one partner to let the other make the major decisions.

"David was very understanding of how I felt about my Presbyterian upbringing," said Anne, "and was very willing to have the ceremony done in my church by my minister. We went to talk with him, and he made us both feel at home. He was thrilled to have the opportunity to participate in our ceremony. That made David feel very comfortable and made it easier for him to accept being married in a Christian ceremony."

"I still asked the minister if he could not talk about Jesus during the ceremony, since I knew that would upset my parents and the members of my family who would be there, and he said that would be no problem," added David. "It turned out that my parents were a lot less upset than I had expected. They were at least glad that I had someone who really loved me and wanted to make me happy.

"They did tell me they were disappointed that I didn't feel that Judaism was important enough to pass on to my children, and felt like they had somehow failed in my upbringing. I didn't really understand why, since they never seemed particularly religious to me. They only went to temple once a year on the High Holidays, and that always seemed sort of hypocritical to me.

"They were as helpful as I could expect when it came to planning the ceremony. After all, it was in Boston and they live outside of Chicago, so they were pretty far away. They did help with some of the expenses when we needed it, but mostly it was Anne's family that was involved. Her mother was thrilled after I agreed to use her minister and her church, and she basically planned the wedding along with Anne."

"It was a nice, warm, loving way to start our married life I think," Anne added. "Everybody seemed to get along real well at the wedding, although there were only a small number of people from the groom's side of the family there. We enjoyed the wedding a lot."

Adam, forty-one and Jewish, married Christy, thirty-four and Protestant, in a synagogue with a rabbi officiating. They made the choice based on a number of factors, including the fact that her parents lived in Hawaii, and it was simply easier to do it in California since his family belonged to a synagogue where the rabbi officiates at interfaith marriages.

"I wanted a religious ceremony," Christy said, "but I didn't really care what kind. We ended up doing it in the temple, but we took out some of the overtly Jewish trappings like the huppah [wedding canopy].

"I suppose what I ended up with was his mother's version of a wedding, since she and the temple and their friends did almost all of the planning. It was a bit difficult for us since we were living in Alaska at the time and were so far away from the wedding site. I wasn't sure what was traditional in a Reform Jewish ceremony, but I wanted *some* of my own ideas in my own wedding."

"We basically let the rabbi do the ceremony," Adam added. "He knew my family very well, and we had met him on several occasions in the past, so he had a good sense of the whole situation. I thought he did a wonderful job of juggling all the various concerns of our families, and Christy's family was pleased in the end, too."

"Adam's mother can get a little berserk at times wanting everything to be exactly *her* way," Christy said. "Fortunately his dad kept her in check and kept reminding her that it was our wedding, not hers."

As you can see, the decisions that individual couples make often have more to do with logistics, distance, and which of their parents feel more strongly about *their* religion, than they have to do with the couples' religious feelings themselves.

It is rare to find *both* partners in an interfaith marriage equally involved and determined to assert their respective religious identities. This was the case for Max and Cindy. Max was just as committed to having his Jewishness represented in the ceremony as Cindy was about her Christianity. They wanted to create a ceremony together that would incorporate elements from both traditions and allow both families to feel equally religiously validated.

In order to accomplish their goal, they spoke to numerous rabbis and ministers until they found two clergy who would agree to co-officiate at their wedding. This was no easy task, since the vast majority of clergy will not participate in a wedding ceremony with clergy of another faith.

They were fortunate that their wedding was taking place in a large metropolitan center where there were enough rabbis and ministers that two who were willing to work together could be found.

They met individually with both the rabbi and the minister, shared their ideas about what they wanted in the ceremony, and listened to the suggestions that each offered from their professional experiences. After they had agreed on the basic thrust of the ceremony itself and the important elements that they wanted to be sure were included, the two clergy spoke directly with each other and worked out the final details.

"It was wonderful," Cindy beamed. "Everyone kept commenting on how beautiful and sensitive the ceremony was for months afterward. In fact, I still get a warm glow inside and a smile on my face whenever I think of it."

"I must admit," said Max, "that it turned out much better than I had thought it would. Everything just seemed to flow so well, and the rabbi and minister worked beautifully together. Both religious traditions were present, everyone knew that we were celebrating both our love for each other *and* the separate traditions with which we were raised, and I think they appreciated the integrity and honesty of it all."

For Max and Cindy the process of weaving their two traditions together was just another expression of their ability to see themselves as *copartners* in everything related to their relationship. They both felt strongly about their respective religions and were willing to have elements of the other's religion included in their wedding. Most of the time, however, one religion takes precedence and is clearly dominant.

"There was no question for me that if there was to be a ceremony at all, it would be a Jewish ceremony," Pam, thirty-eight, told me. "Part of it probably has to do with the fact that my parents are survivors of the Holocaust. I knew that they would die if I married without a Jewish ceremony, and I just couldn't do that to them. Arthur was very understanding of my needs and never once disagreed with my decision.

"My parents are so 'old world' in their thinking that my mother even told all her friends that Arthur had converted before the ceremony, even though she knows that he didn't. She was embarrassed in front of her Jewish friends that I had married a non-Jew and couldn't stand to have them think I'd somehow abandoned Judaism by marrying Arthur."

"I really had no feelings at all about it since my own religious background was practically nil," Arthur said. "Whatever Pam wanted was fine with me. As long as I could make everyone happy just by agreeing to a particular ceremony, I thought that was an easy way to be a hero in the family."

Arthur discovered something that is true for many interfaith weddings: Saying yes to the wishes of your partner's family is a simple, yet powerful way to leave a lasting positive impression about your concern and care for the feelings of your in-laws. This can be a wonderful way to begin a marriage, since the goodwill it generates can help set the stage for a lifetime of positive feelings.

Often planning an interfaith wedding is so fraught with tension that the solution the couple ultimately chooses is flight.

"I called some rabbis at first and got negative responses to my inquiry about performing our marriage," Ruth told me. "My father refused at first to even meet my husband, although my mother did. In the end we just had to put on our own wedding, so we got married on a ship with a captain. We wrote our own prayers and vows, selected music, and tried to include different elements of both religions and traditions in the service.

"The only thing that I didn't want was any mention of Jesus in my wedding. He promised me that he wouldn't do it, and then he did it anyway, but I didn't let it ruin the wedding for me, because we had created a beautiful ceremony in our own neutral place."

Monica, forty-three and Catholic, and Bill, forty-five and Jewish, split the difference between their two religions in an attempt at striking a compromise that wouldn't allow one side or the other to dominate.

"We decided to get married in a Unitarian church," Monica said. "It turned out to be a kind of compromise position for both of us, since at the time we both felt strongly about not getting married in the other's religious place."

"I didn't want to be married in a Catholic church," Bill said. "It made me very uncomfortable just to think about it. She didn't want a temple, either, so we tried to find a nondenominational setting that was still somehow religious in overtone."

"In the end I think it also cut down the tension between our families and the guests," Monica added. "All the time I'm sure they were wondering how each side would react to one setting or the other, and this was neutral ground for everyone. Besides, in the Catholic faith there was a long procedure to go through if we had wanted a Catholic wedding, and it just wasn't worth it to me to push for that."

Sometimes it works out that the clergy person that the couple likes turns out to be from one of their own religious backgrounds. Such was the case with Jack and Diane.

When discussing their wedding with me, Jack said, "We always had quick weddings in my family where people would run off to Vegas for the ceremony. We had seen a rabbi marry some friends and we loved him and the ceremony. I cried at the ceremony of my friends it was so moving, so we decided that was who we wanted to marry us.

"It wasn't really because he was Jewish or a rabbi, but it worked out well that way. The ceremony was filled with love and joy, and we were both really touched. If he'd been a Buddhist priest we would have still wanted him, just for the kind of ceremony that he did."

"It helped a lot with my family to have a rabbi marrying us," Diane added. "We were just lucky that the one person whose ceremony we fell in love with turned out to be a rabbi, because that made my parents very happy, and it seemed to be a good choice in the end for most people involved.

"We discussed having two clergy do it together to please his parents, too. I'd expected not to marry a Jewish man all along, so I'd thought about it in advance and had seen a two-clergy wedding and liked it. But we found that there would be more problems trying to find the two than just using the rabbi that we liked anyway, so that's what we did. He was wonderful all alone, and everyone felt comfortable and at ease with his ceremony, so it was a good choice in the end."

Deciding Where the Ceremony Will Be

Deciding upon where the ceremony will take place is often as difficult as choosing what the ceremony itself will be like. The challenge is to find a place that will make you happy, while at the same time not offending either set of parents, or even preventing someone from attending.

In choosing a wedding site the most important consideration ought to be what will make *you* happy. Remembering that this is *your* wedding is one of the greatest challenges in any couple's wedding planning, and is particularly important in an interfaith wedding.

There is no "right" answer to any of the myriad wedding decisions that you will make. I have participated in hundreds of weddings, and they have been as varied as the individuals were. Whether the wedding takes place in a religious institution, a hotel, country club, private home, on the beach, by a lake, in the mountains, at a camp, on a ship, in a restaurant, or on the 18th hole of a golf course, the essential thing is that *you* make the decision based upon *your* relationship and what is best for it.

It is always a good idea to take parents' needs into consideration, but in the end, when the ceremony is over and the guests and parents go home, you will be (fortunately) left with each other. It will be the two of you who will be looking back on your wedding day and smiling or cringing, so do all you can to have it in a place that will make the two of you happy.

When Parents Say They Won't Come

One of the most emotionally devastating experiences for many young couples who are planning an interfaith marriage is the moment when they receive the news that one or more of their parents refuses to come to the wedding.

When parents are confronted with the news that their son or daughter has decided to marry someone of a different religion, it is not unusual for their emotional reaction to take over and obscure the possibility of a rational, dispassionate response. They simply have too many years' worth of emotion invested in being "right" about their religious beliefs, practices, and associations to allow for the acceptance of something different as being equally valid, especially for their child.

It is often a very painful reality to confront for interfaith couples, and one for which they are not totally prepared. Time and time again I have sat with young people who shook their heads in disbelief as they recounted the shock they had experienced when their parents exploded in overt rejection of their marriage, their mate, and themselves.

"I just didn't know what to say," Ben told me, "when my parents started yelling at me. I was in shock. I guess I just never thought about the possibility that they would be so upset. They weren't that religious when I was growing up, so it never occurred to me that they would have such strong feelings about whom I married.

"When I told them that Sally and I had decided to get married, I expected what everyone expects, that my parents would be happy for me and glad that I had found someone to love and share my life with. It was a shock to find out how they really felt, and it plugged me right back into being their little boy again who wanted their approval—it was terrible."

"I wasn't very thrilled about it myself," Sally added. "I felt like there was something wrong with me. I had always been raised to be tolerant and accepting of other people and their differences, and so had Ben. That's why it seemed so strange to both of us that his parents reacted so violently to the idea of our marriage—it just didn't fit with his upbringing."

The experiences of Sally and Ben are not unique. All too often couples discover that the lessons their parents taught them about pluralism, tolerance, all people being equal and worthy of respect and the like, were really political positions directed at the broad issues of society, and not intended to be taken into their own bedroom.

When parents say they won't come to your wedding, it presents you with some difficult choices to make. I have never known a situation, although it may happen, in which the decision of parents not to attend their child's wedding changed their child's mind or prevented the marriage from taking place. Instead, it merely causes pain and grief to everyone involved.

So what do you do when your parents say they aren't coming? The first thing to do is to sit down and consider what your options are. There are three obvious possible reactions that you might have: (1) cancel the wedding, (2) do it exactly as you have planned, and (3) change the ceremony in some way in an attempt to appease your parents.

Regardless of what you actually end up doing, I strongly recommend a face to face meeting with your parents. It is very difficult to reaffirm and strengthen the natural bonds of love and affection between you and your parents over the phone. If they live in New York and you live in San Francisco, get on the next plane going east.

This accomplishes a number of important objectives. First, it tells them in very concrete terms that they are very important to you. It lets them know without question that you haven't simply abandoned them and their beliefs for another family and culture, but that they are still and will always be an unreplaceable and important part of your life.

Second, it gives you the opportunity to reestablish the parent/child bond that may have become worn through the years. It is easy when you no longer live with your parents for their fantasies of what you are doing and how you are living your life to become a barrier between you. The physical distance becomes an emotional distance as well, and often only your physical presence back in the family fold once again can overcome that distance.

Third, it lets them know that you take their feelings and thoughts very seriously, and that you truly want them to understand *your* feelings as well. You can sit and discuss how you each feel about your decision to marry someone of another religion, and at the same time emphasize that it is not necessarily a rejection of either them or your upbringing.

Very often I have seen this face to face encounter break down the barriers of resistance and allow parents to overcome their initial rejection. This is especially so when they see that you are respectful of their feelings, pained over the emotional and physical distance between them and you, *and* secure and firm about your love for and decision to marry your fiancé.

It often takes a confrontation with both the reality of the decision and the maturity with which you have approached it to bring parents around to an emotional place where they are willing to accept and be a part of your wedding.

Most parents do not want to lose touch with their children. They do not want to lose your love either, and usually when you reinforce how much you love and care about them, while maintaining your own status as an adult who makes his or her own decisions, they come around.

Unfortunately, there are still those cases in which the parents simply refuse to have anything to do with the wedding. Beyond what I have already suggested, there is little that can be done to change their mind, unless you are willing to change *your* decision and marry someone else.

You can take some comfort in knowing that most of the time the yelling and screaming, the attempts at derailing your wedding plans, the attacks and open disapproval all cease after the wedding has actually taken place. Even though their rejection can be painful, and even embarrassing in front of someone you love, remember that subconsciously they know that if they are to have any chance of preventing you from making what they consider to be a big mistake, it can only happen *before* the wedding.

Underneath it all is a love and caring for you that in part is motivating their rejection of your marriage. Put yourself in their place for a moment and assume that they love you and think you are making a bad decision. The natural thing for them to do in that instance is whatever they can to prevent you from doing irreparable harm to yourself.

Since most parents change their attitude and response after the marriage actually takes place, it is important to do your best not to cut off your relationship with them while planning the wedding. Keep your cool. Tell them you are hurt and sorry that they won't be at your wedding since you love them and really want them to be there.

Tell them that you hope they will feel different after they come to know the person you love, and that you see your relationship as an expression of the very values they taught you. After you have shared your feelings with them, made it clear (without shouting, name-calling, or rejecting them) that you still intend to marry this person and only want what is natural, namely, to have your parents share in your joyous occasion, that is all you can do.

Let them make their own decision while you allow the possibility of a relationship with them when tempers have cooled (and tell them that is what you are doing). Then you and your partner need to discuss the situation together so that she/he doesn't take your parents' rejection as a personal insult which may prevent any future relationship from developing.

Parental rejection is one of the most painful and difficult aspects of interfaith marriage. Unfortunately, short of therapy, your parents' going through their own process of self-examination, or perhaps giving them this book to read, you can do very little. Just keep the door open for the future, let whatever rejection there is come from them and not you, and most likely they too will come around when the marriage is a reality.

Attitude Is the Key to Peace of Mind

Families are not all the same. Since each family has its own peculiarities and needs, I have seen situations time and again in which the bride and groom felt compelled, for the sake of making or keeping peace within the larger family, to give in to parents on any number of individual aspects of the wedding itself.

If this is unavoidable, do it gracefully, with the attitude that you are freely *choosing* to allow your parents to make certain decisions. Attitude becomes the key to your peace of mind, and to the total manner in which you actually experience your wedding.

Attitude is the one thing over which you have absolute control; it is the single most powerful tool you have at your command. Use it to your advantage, and when you see no way out, create the attitude that *you* are choosing to have it be the way it is anyway— try it and see what a liberating experience it is.

After you have mastered the ability to take control of your own attitude about life, you will realize how easy it is to create the joy, satisfaction, and fulfillment that you desire, even in the midst of events that otherwise seem out of your control.

Sometimes those who elope to escape the pressures of parental involvement in their relationship and in their wedding plans are cheating themselves of the chance to set an important pattern *not only* for themselves, but for their parents and family as well. While it may be the only solution to an untenable situation, running off to get married alone is often seen by others as an inability to stand up and say to the world, "We are proud of our relationship; we love each other and want to share what we have together with those we love in our lives."

A wedding is a time to demonstrate to your family that you are united in your love, united in your support for each other, and united in your commitment to each other. It can also demonstrate that you are united in your ability to say, *"Our* relationship comes first. If we can make others happy we will, but if there is a conflict, we know that our relationship is the most important thing to both of us and will always take precedence."

Planning a wedding is a stress-filled time for everyone, regardless of the religion, regardless of the family situation, regardless of the ages of the couple. It is a time of great excitement, of looking toward the future with delight, of anticipating the years of joy that come from sharing a life with someone you love.

It is also a time filled with a thousand decisions, each of which seems to grow larger in direct proportion to the difficulty in reaching agreement among the bride, groom, and involved family members. As if simply making these decisions wasn't hard enough, parents and even grandparents get into the act with an unlimited supply of free advice as to exactly how you should be planning *your* wedding.

They will tell you who should be invited, who should *not* be invited, where it should be held, who should officiate at the ceremony, the kind of food you should serve, the clothes you should wear, the way your hair should look, where you should go on a honeymoon, what kind of music should be played, when it should start, who should walk down the aisle first, second, third, fourth, and last, where you should buy your rings, the kind of flowers you should have, where the guests should be seated, who should definitely *not* sit next to whom, the kind of veil you should wear, the length of your dress, the *only* place to buy invitations, and who should serve as your best man and maid of honor, just for starters.

Trying to deflect the constant waves of well-intentioned advice from relatives is itself a full-time job. The only way you can make it through this jungle of suggestions in one piece is to have a firm and steady hand to hold on to. *That* hand needs to be on the end of your mate's arm, and it needs to be held tightly in yours as you go about deciding *together* what your wedding will ultimately look like.

In fact, if you want to run away to Las Vegas, then by all means *go* hand in hand into the desert, but just as Moses returned from *his* desert trip with the proverbial commandments etched in stone, so too, you should return from *your* sojourn with your wedding plans carved into the pillars of your relationship so permanently that not even the most persistent mother-in-law would dare to change a word.

Ultimately, whether your wedding becomes a source of upset and discord or an opportunity to demonstrate the love and support in your relationship is in your hands. Others can argue with both of you, but only *you* can argue with each other.

Take the strategies that others have shared with us to heart. Listen to their cautions, and learn from their successes.

Be a team. Use the keys of communication and cooperation to unlock the secret door to a successful wedding experience for you and your spouse. Put yourself in control, choose to give specific decisions to others as *you* see fit, and you will create a wedding to look back on with pride and satisfaction.

Chapter VII

CONVERSION

"I decided to convert, because after my experiences growing up in a house filled with religious conflict, I didn't want to go through that in *my* house with my kids."

—Mary, raised by Catholic father and Protestant mother

Sharon and Tom had already been married for five years when I first met them at an anniversary party for mutual friends, whom I had married five years earlier.

When they heard that a rabbi who was writing a book on interfaith marriage was at the party, they made a point of coming over to talk with me. Sharon thought that I would be interested in her story, and what she told me turned out to be both fascinating and enlightening.

Sharon was raised in a Catholic family, but had stopped going to church of her own volition in her early teens. It wasn't that she had any strong feelings about Catholicism one way or another, it was simply that religion had never been that important to her.

By the time she was in her early twenties, she was working in a real estate office, living on her own, and at most attending church with her parents once or twice a year, at Christmas and Easter.

She met Tom at the office, and they quickly developed mutual caring, trust, and rapport. She found that she loved being with him and looked forward to seeing him every day. Over the next year and a half, their relationship grew and blossomed into a deep and abiding love. They seemed to be compatible in almost every area of their lives, and the fact that Tom was Jewish and she was Catholic didn't seem to be much of a barrier to either of them.

Sharon told me that at the time they first discussed getting married, they decided that since Tom felt more strongly about his Judaism than she did about her Catholicism, she would do whatever she could to help him celebrate Jewish holidays as he always had in the past.

The idea of conversion never really came up, since Tom was very comfortable with the life-style that they had together and saw no reason for anything to change. Sharon continued to go to Christmas and Easter Mass with her parents, and celebrated the High Holidays, Hanukkah, and Passover with Tom's parents and family.

When they had their first child, a girl, three years later, at Tom's request she was given a Hebrew name in the local synagogue.

As Sharon told it, "All along I was feeling increasingly caught in a strange emotional bind. On the one hand, everything was very easy for me, since I felt no pressure from Tom or his family to be any different than I had always been. On the other hand, as I experienced more and more of Tom's Jewish world and allowed myself and my child to be involved with it as well, I began to feel that there was an artificial gap between us with Tom Jewish, me sort of Catholic, and the baby I didn't know what.

"What eventually happened was that four years after we were married, completely on my own, I announced to Tom one day that I wanted to convert to Judaism."

"I was really pleasantly surprised," Tom said. "I knew that Sharon didn't have particularly strong feelings about being Catholic, but we had never discussed conversion before—I was satisfied with the life we were leading, and Sharon just always seemed to fit in."

"What did it for me in the end was a feeling of estrangement from Tom, in a subtle kind of way. It was like we were doing the same things, sharing the same experiences, but I was doing them as an outsider and he was on the inside. I suppose it sounds silly, since no one certainly ever *made* me feel that way, but I did anyway.

"I kept thinking that as our life continued and our baby began to grow up, she would want to know who and what she was. I didn't like the idea that she would grow up in a family that was somehow divided and not entirely whole and integrated. I also felt that choosing Judaism would be an act of deeper connection with Tom, almost a symbol of closing the gap between us and totally integrating our lives—and that's exactly how it has felt."

After Sharon made the initial decision, she enrolled in an Introduction to Judaism class at a local synagogue with Tom. They found that studying together did in fact give them an added sense of connection and helped bridge the distance that was a natural part of being raised in two different religions.

After Sharon and Tom shared their story with me, I discovered that according to a study of the American Jewish Committee, almost forty percent of those who convert to Judaism do so *after* they are married, and nearly twenty-five percent convert after the birth of their first child. It seems that Sharon was neither the first nor the only person involved in an interfaith marriage to make the choice of conversion years after her marriage began.

What is important for our discussion is for you to look upon conversion as simply one of the available strategies for coping with the complexities of interfaith marriage. For those who find it appropriate, given their own personal history and emotional needs, it becomes an important expression of their desire to be united in as many ways as possible.

Conversion isn't right for everyone, and as you can see from the dozens of happily married couples that you are meeting throughout the pages of this book, it doesn't appear to be a necessary component of a happy interfaith relationship. I know that some of you are thinking: "Why is this in a book on interfaith marriage in the first place, since if someone converts to the other's religion, then they have the *same* faith, and strictly speaking are no longer involved in an interfaith marriage at all?"

Well, you are right. Yet, the very fact that so many marriages *begin* as interfaith marriages, even if they don't end up that way, is reason enough to include this as one of the important options to think about as you contemplate the best way for you to deal with your own relationship.

The subject of conversion can provoke a great deal of emotion on both sides. Often, pressure to convert begins with one partner's parents, and it can get to be quite annoying and divisive if it is allowed to continue unchecked.

"His mother was dying for me to convert and would say something about it every time we were alone," Janie, who was raised as a Protestant and married a Catholic, told me. "She started to tell me, 'It's time to convert already . . .' about two days after I first met her, and it really made me nervous. His sister came to my defense and got her off of me. I wasn't ready to discuss it at the time. It takes some time to develop those feelings, if you ever do, and my mother-in-law on my back only made me more resistant to the idea."

Many times, even when there is an inclination to convert, people don't do it because they don't want to hurt their own parents' feelings. As with every aspect of your life together, you will constantly be faced with decisions that are potentially alienating to your family or that of your partner. Establishing an appropriate balance in your life between your needs and the needs of others who are important to you is one of the great ongoing challenges of an interfaith marriage.

Andy, who was raised as a Congregationalist, married Michelle, who is Jewish. He has become very involved in their synagogue, celebrates Jewish holidays, is sending their child to a Jewish religious school, and basically feels very much a part of the Jewish community and world.

He has chosen, however, *not* to formally convert to Judaism, and like many others to remain what I call a Jew by association. His reasons are typical of many who are involved in interfaith relationships, and it may help those of you who are in the same situation to hear what he had to say.

"I don't feel like I have to make a decision right away about formal conversion, regardless of how I act or feel. I already participate as fully in synagogue life as anyone else does—but I am also concerned about alienating my parents whom I love very much. It would kill them if I converted away from the way *they* raised me, and away from *their* beliefs. I just can't do that to them, regardless of what I personally believe.

"After they are no longer here, I will be able to think about a formal conversion, but not before. The only way I could ever do it now is if I converted and never told them, but I don't think I would feel right about that from any point of view. When I do it, I want to do it all the way, and openly, but not while my parents are alive."

Andy's comments are typical of large numbers of interfaith couples who feel trapped between their own beliefs, feelings, and life-style, and the feelings and sensitivities of their parents. The personal rejection that parents often feel when children choose to live their lives within a tradition that is different from the way they were raised is a serious and important reason why many simply never take that step in any formal ceremony.

Rejecting formal conversion can be an honest and caring response to the feelings and needs of our parents, even as we assert our own independent right as adults to give expression to what is important to *us*.

Whichever decision you make in your life, let it be an honest one. Conversion to another religion is a big step and obviously not to be taken lightly or for someone else. It is an intensely personal experience and usually grows out of a process of introspection and self-examination, as well as the opportunity to experience the new religion of choice firsthand in your daily life.

Yes, there are benefits to conversion. These include a religiously unified family, a lack of possible confusion or competition with children between one parent's religion and the other's, a greater sense of communality with your spouse, a shared vision of the world and the place of godliness and spirituality in your lives, the opportunity to build an ever-greater sense of common purpose and shared meaning in your life together, the ability to share common rituals, holidays, and celebrations, and more.

Above all, when one partner converts to the religion of the other, there is often an added unidentifiable bond that grows between them. It is a quiet, gentle joining together of lives and spirits in common purpose that transcends personal histories and binds the couple together as part of a larger world family of common faith. For many, this added sense of being part of the same larger family is the most wonderful side benefit that conversion offers.

In addition to all the above, there are statistics that seem to indicate that the chance of an interfaith marriage's failing are up to six times greater than a same-faith marriage. Choosing to adopt the religion of your spouse changes the marriage from interfaith to same-faith, and many thousands of couples each year choose this option as the optimum way to avoid the pains and problems of living and raising children in an interfaith environment.

Statistics seem to demonstrate that same-faith marriages have a better chance of marital happiness and success, and present less stress and conflict for children and a more stable and secure religious environment in which to grow. This is why many see conversion as the best way to increase the chances of creating a satisfying, nurturing, and loving relationship.

In every community there are churches and synagogues that offer Introduction to _____ classes, and formal conversion courses. If you feel that choosing to adopt the religion of your partner is an option worth looking into, speak to the appropriate clergy person in your local church or synagogue, and they will guide you in the right direction. If for some reason the first person you speak with doesn't meet your needs, or doesn't seem sympathetic to your situation, don't give up, just keep searching until you find someone who is.

The Difficulties of Conversion

In the midst of this discussion about the benefits of conversion, let me share some caveats as well. Conversion is not a quick fix for a sagging relationship. It is not a tool to manipulate your wife or husband, mother-in-law or father-in-law, into liking or accepting you more.

Conversion must be a heartfelt experience, entered into with your whole being—honestly, sincerely, because *you* want it to be. Too often people have "agreed" to conversion in order to please a potential spouse or in-law, primarily because their most important goal is simply getting married, and this seems like the necessary spiritual fee to get into their own wedding.

Making such a decision is asking for disaster. It is placing yourself in the vulnerable position of having sacrificed something of *you* on the altar of your relationship. The almost inevitable result will be a buildup of resentment toward the very person you are trying to create a relationship with in the first place.

Your partner loves you for who you are, not because you are willing to sacrifice your own religion for hers/his. Furthermore, what kind of respect could he or she have for their own religion if they think so little of it that they would expect someone to formally convert to it without even really understanding or believing it in the first place?

More than anything else, such a request is probably an indication of a lack of religious sensitivity and understanding on the part of your partner. It is a sign of religious immaturity, for it indicates that in your partner's eyes, appearances are more important than substance.

Take your time. Read as many books as you can on the new religion, speak with clergy and lay representatives of that religious body, subscribe to religious journals that grow out of that particular denomination, sect, or religious group, and listen to speakers and tapes. But most important is to *live* the religion in all its manifestations so as to truly integrate the religion and its practices into your life. Then you can make a choice based not on ignorance and stereotype, not out of expediency or pressure, but out of a shared understanding and the personal experiences of being together in a religious environment that *you* find adds meaning and purpose to your life.

An additional reason *not* to convert merely so that you will be accepted by others, whether it be your spouse or your spouse's family, is that often it simply doesn't work anyway. Take for example the story of Fran and Michael. Fran was raised Catholic but converted to Judaism prior to her marriage to Michael. "After we talked about it a lot," she told me, "I realized that he felt much more strongly about his religion than I did, so going to a church seemed hypocritical to me and I stopped. By the time we actually decided to get married, I wanted our kids to be all one religion.

"His side of the family gave him lots of pressure about our marriage. Two of his uncles even offered to send him to Israel to get him away from me so he could meet a nice Jewish girl. His mother cried to him all the time that he was doing something terrible, and here *I* was converting to *their* religion!

"When I called *my* parents, who *should* have been upset, they turned out to be very supportive. We ended up having a nice traditional Jewish wedding, all because my Catholic mother put it on for us, and the kicker is, his parents *still* didn't come to the wedding."

"Yes," Michael admitted, "I was really embarrassed by the whole thing. Here she was going out of her way to be accommodating for me, and her parents were going along with it, and *mine* would neither come to the wedding nor have anything to do with her. I was angry as can be at them, as you can well imagine."

One of the lessons that can be learned from experiences like these is the importance of truly knowing that *you* are the most important person in your partner's life. When family members become totally unreasonable, as I believe Michael's parents were, they are both driving a wedge between their child and themselves and driving the interfaith couple even closer together.

In fact, many couples believe that the hostility and resistance that they felt from their parents, particularly when it involved a rejection of an intended conversion, helped them solidify their feelings for each other. It reminded them that the only people they could really count on for support and love were each other, and in general it became a force for strengthening their relationship.

On the other hand, one might learn an entirely different lesson from the story of Fran and Michael. Fran's conversion seemed to be primarily out of a desire to unify her family into one religion and make Michael happy.

Michael's parents may simply have been reflecting their reading of her intentions, and the conviction that her conversion was one of expedience rather than commitment and belief. They might have felt that conversion merely for the sake of unity in the home was not truly a conversion at all, but merely a change of external label.

Their way of handling the situation was in any event abominable, but their appraisal and rejection of Fran's conversion might not have been totally off base. When challenged with this particular interpretation of her actions, Fran responded that discovering her true religious feelings happened as a result both of discussions with Michael about his religion and of her willingness to participate in an Introduction to Judaism class. This particular experience helped her to clarify her beliefs and ultimately to choose conversion to Judaism as the path her life would follow.

In fact, only because she was so secure in her conversion and her sense of identity as a Jew was she able to transcend the emotional slap in the face that she received from her in-laws for so long. She told me, "It bothered me at first, since I felt I had done something important and special, and it was *their* religion anyway, and they still didn't accept me in the family.

"After a while, I realized that I didn't convert for them, or even for Michael. Ultimately, I converted for myself. I knew this for sure the moment I realized that if for some reason Michael and I ever ended our relationship, I would always be Jewish anyway, because that's just who I am now. It felt good to know that the changes within me are both permanent and significant in my life."

Choosing to share the religion of your partner is an important step in any relationship, and one not to be taken lightly. Do it for you. Do it because it's the only thing you *can* do to remain true to yourself and your own beliefs and feelings.

Whether you choose to convert to your partner's religion or not, it is the strength of the relationship itself, the love you share, your willingness to share your feelings and needs openly and honestly with each other, that will determine the ultimate success of your interfaith marriage.

Chapter VIII

TYING THE KNOT

"At the wedding the minister showed up with robes and crosses on a shawl, and I didn't want to offend my family. In fact, I even asked a rabbi to participate, but he wouldn't. So the minister took off the crosses, and then it looked secular and everyone liked it and thought it was beautiful."

—Richard, thirty-eight, Jewish,
interfaith married six years

_____

So you're finally getting married. It's probably not today, or tomorrow, since most people don't read books like this on the day of their wedding, but it may be coming up sooner than you think, and you are beginning to suffer from what are traditionally known as last-minute jitters. You may even be plagued with a few doubts about the whole enterprise now that it is almost upon you. Don't despair, there's nothing wrong with you, for last-minute doubts are a common experience.

Think about it for a moment and you will realize, if you are like most interfaith couples, that there have probably been a number of emotionally draining experiences and encounters before you have gotten to the point where the actual wedding itself is looming on the horizon. With all the stress and strain that so often accompany interfaith marriages, it is little wonder that at certain moments you begin to ask yourself, "Is it really worth it? Is this what my life is going to be like forever, constantly having to "handle" one situation or another, assuage one or another parent's hurt feelings? Maybe I should have just married a _____."

Chances are the answers to all the above questions are yes. Yes, you will probably still feel that it is all worth it, if you truly love the person you are about to marry and have worked through in advance with him or her the many decisions, questions, understandings, and issues that are part of an interfaith relationship.

Yes, this is in one form or another what your life is going to be like forever. You have chosen a path that will find you constantly dealing with the feelings of in-laws and extended family members, constantly having to make decisions about whether and how to celebrate religious holidays and events, and if so with whom and in what way, constantly having to consciously work at communicating with the one you love in the most open, supportive, honest, and understanding way possible.

So with it all perhaps, yes, it would have been better to marry someone with the same religious background as you. *But,* you are going to marry *this* real, live, flesh and blood human being with whom you have fallen in love, pledged loyalty and life, and are preparing to create a future and build a family of your own.

It's natural to have last-minute doubts, and it can often be helpful to you as well. Now that you have them, use them. Take the next few moments, or hours, or even days, to reaffirm your commitment to this impending marriage.

If you have questions, explore them. Explore them with someone you trust: talk to your best friend about them, talk to an outside neutral party or therapist about them, and above all, talk to your loved one about them. After all, this is the person who is to become, if he/she isn't already, your best friend and confidant, the one with whom you share your innermost secrets and fears and will continue to do so for the rest of your life. If you aren't comfortable sharing your doubts and emotional struggles with the person you are about to marry, then they may be justified after all.

Trust yourself and your feelings, for you are your own best therapist. Most problems come when people get carried away with decisions that they have made, simply because they already made them, and ignore the inner voice that whispers the truth in their own ears.

Be courageous enough to confront your doubts and your decisions honestly. Chances are your last-minute questions and fears are just that, natural expressions of all the tension and stress that may have been a part of the whole process up to now, and nothing more.

Often, even individuals who are about to enter into a same-faith marriage have doubts, anxieties, questions, and hesitancies about taking such an important step as marriage. Don't think that your experience is simply a result of the interfaith nature of your relationship. However, it is also important to trust yourself enough to know when the doubts are founded on something substantial enough to make you reconsider the decision in the first place.

Weddings do have a momentum all their own, and once you start the ball rolling, once people have been invited, arrangements made, millions of decisions agreed upon, it becomes almost impossible to stop. That doesn't mean that people don't call off weddings; it happens all the time. It just reflects a reality that doing so is often a *very* difficult thing to do, emotionally *and* logistically.

Still, if you do feel in the end that for whatever reason you have made a mistake, it is far better to go through the emotional trauma of calling the wedding off than to put yourself through a dishonest wedding and the inevitable greater pain and suffering of a divorce down the road.

If you are still reading on after that gloomy thought, let me reassure you once again that most people *do* have moments of doubt and question prior to their actual wedding. So don't despair, just confront them honestly and count on yourself to make the right decisions for you.

"His/Her Parents Will Never Like Me"

Charlotte was a victim of what I call the "His/her parents will never like me" syndrome. When there has been some tension and disapproval expressed by someone's parents prior to the marriage, parental approval can become one of the tender areas within the relationship.

"I remember the entire week before the wedding saying to myself with a sense of impending doom and despair, 'His parents will *never* like me,' and imagining this endless lifetime of trying to please them and change their minds all the time," thirty-six-year-old Charlotte told me one day. "It was awful. Here I was about to get married to Ron, whom I really loved a lot, and I was worrying all the time about his parents.

"I thought I must be going nuts. I kept reminding myself that I was marrying Ron, not his parents, and I was smart enough to talk to him about it, so that by the time we got to the wedding itself, I was back in tune with all the love and support that he represented in my life, and I let go of the anxiety of his parents' difficulty in accepting me as their daughter-in-law."

"I was glad that she said something about it," Ron said. "I knew that she was upset about something, but you know, before a wedding I figured it could be anything. I finally asked if there was anything I could do to make her feel better or more comfortable about what we were doing. Then she told me what she was really thinking about, and we had the chance to talk it out."

Along with the concern about parental approval often comes anxiety about the ceremony itself, particularly when it is going to be performed by a clergy person of one faith or the other that is new and unfamiliar to the bride or groom. Anxiety over the ceremony is one area where interfaith couples often displace and redirect their anxiety over the marriage itself, so it's important to monitor exactly where the source of concern that *you* feel may be coming from as *your* ceremony approaches.

Sit down with the person performing the ceremony in advance. Ask her or him to go over the ceremony, to explain exactly what will happen, the meaning and significance of any rituals or symbols, in as much detail as possible. I have found that when I explain exactly to the bride and groom what will be happening in the ceremony, go over it point by point, discuss what I say and why with them, their anxiety usually disappears.

Be assertive about your wedding. If the person performing the ceremony tells you something that you are uncomfortable with, speak up and see if he/she will change it. Most clergy who participate in interfaith weddings are very sensitive to the dynamics of an interfaith marriage. Otherwise, they wouldn't be performing the wedding in the first place.

Interfaith marriage is a much-discussed topic at clergy conferences and meetings, and there are numerous approaches to the event itself that are possible. As I have said before, it's *your* wedding, just as it is your marriage, and you have a right to be satisfied and happy with the content of the ceremony.

Most clergy are delighted to have suggestions from the couple as to the kind of things they would like in their ceremony. After all, we are there to serve you, to make sure that your wedding is as emotionally satisfying a way to begin the married part of your life together as possible. So don't be afraid to question, suggest, and try out ideas—it may be the only way you will have to get the kind of ceremony that you want.

The Wedding Is Not the Marriage

It's important to remember through all the tension and potential upset that surrounds the actual wedding itself that the wedding is *not* your marriage. Your marriage is the daily living of your loving relationship as you go about the task of creating a life together. The wedding is simply the ceremony that you share with your family and friends to announce your love and commitment to each other, and your intention to spend your life together in this special sanctified relationship.

The wedding may be fraught with tensions all its own that have nothing whatsoever to do with your relationship, your love for one another, your plans for your life together, or the ease and comfort with which you live together. Fortunately, most couples don't *live* afterward with the people who come to the wedding. It's easy to get swept away with the emotion of the moment, particularly on your wedding day itself, when emotions tend to run high. Take a few deep breaths and remember why you are there in the first place going through with the ceremony. That usually helps reduce the wedding day panics to a minimum and allows you to actually *enjoy* your wedding, which is the idea in the first place.

Coping with Crisis

Okay, it's your wedding day, you are in the bridal room in the church/synagogue/hotel, and someone rushes in to tell you that the yellow three-tiered cake with the red-roses frosting that you ordered just arrived, only it's a green two-tiered monstrosity with pink snapdragons. What do you do?

Handling various potential crises on the day of your wedding can be a major source of anxiety and tension. With all the intricate details that often accompany a wedding ceremony, there are lots of things that might not turn out exactly the way you had envisioned. *Don't panic* is rule number one.

Whatever the possible source of the upset, first take a deep breath and ask yourself, "How important is this particular thing to my happiness today?" If the answer is that you don't really care what color the frosting is, as long as the cake itself is good, or you wanted to have roses in your bouquet, but the orchids they sent will do just fine, then smile and chalk it up to other people's ineptitude and *enjoy* your wedding. It is to be hoped it's the last one you will ever have, so make the most out of it.

Knowing how to cope with a crisis is a skill that can be particularly useful for a bride or groom to possess on a wedding day. There are innumerable opportunities to practice such skills, from the last-minute panic when the minister's car breaks down ten miles out of town on the highway, to the musicians forgetting to show, or a parent's saying they won't even attend the wedding if they don't get to stand next to their son/daughter under the traditional Jewish wedding canopy.

Use each decision as a way of reinforcing your partnership of love with your spouse and providing an example of how you can make decisions together for the good of the relationship. Now more than ever, the very day of the wedding, *talk* to each other and *share* your fears, needs, desires, and emotions. Then the wedding will be a fabulous, emotionally exhilarating experience for both of you.

Before the wedding day, sit down with your parents, the caterer, the bandleader, the clergy person, the wedding coordinator, or whomever, and explain to them what your priorities are, the issues that you do not feel strongly about, and those over which you will simply not compromise. This will pave the way for a smoother resolution of potential problems or special situations that may pop up, since everyone involved will already know what is and is not important to you.

If something gets out of control because you simply *have* no control over it (such as the band calling in late due to three flat tires and an overturned truck on the highway), when all else fails, simply *choose* to have your wedding day turn out the way it is already. Say to yourself, "Well, I guess this is the way my wedding is supposed to be, since this is certainly the way it is."

Smile, take several slow, long, deep breaths, relax, find something about it that is humorous, and laugh. Realize that the most important thing about getting married is the relationship, and the relationship is the same whether the flowers are blue or yellow, or the band plays the wrong song as you walk down the aisle. Concentrate on *why* you are there in the first place and realize that it wasn't simply to organize an award-winning party for relatives you never see and hardly know.

That perspective will get you through many a rough moment, and if you can keep your sense of humor despite the most ridiculous things happening on your wedding day, you will have demonstrated that your true priorities are exactly where they ought to be—with the love of your partner.

Enjoying the Day—Celebrating Your Love

Without question, the single most important thing to remember on your wedding day is *have fun*. It is a celebration of your love for each other, an opportunity to show off your love to the world, to dance and sing and hold each other in your arms all day and night. *Enjoy* the wedding. *Enjoy* the day. Get the very most out of it that you can, so that years from now you can look back on it with fondness, affection, and the warm glow of memory that illuminates one of the truly special moments of your life.

This is the start of a new life together with the one you love. That fact alone ought to be enough to help you transcend the picayune details and irritations that sometimes plague wedding ceremonies. Don't allow them to drag you down, to put a damper on one of the most exciting and important days of your life. It *is* one of the most important days of your life, so live it that way.

A very wise American philosopher, Earle Nightengale, once said, "As you think, so shall you become." And so it is on your wedding day. Whether you are happy or sad, nostalgic or excited about the future, feeling loved or having your feelings hurt, is all a matter of decisions that you make in your mind. You can *decide* to be happy, to accept things exactly the way they are, to celebrate your accomplishments in life, to feel loved by those around you, to experience the thrill of a world filled with friends who really care about you and a partner who loves you for all your qualities, even the ones you aren't particularly thrilled with.

All of this is possible, simply by having the right attitude. It is attitude that determines your total wedding experience, and since it is the one thing that you have total control over yourself, make your attitude work *for* you and not *against* you.

There are innumerable ways to experience being loved by others. Not only is your partner there with you, going through all the same trials and tribulations for only one reason—namely, that he/she loves you—but others are there for that reason as well. Stop if you will, in front of all the assembled guests. Look at their faces, probably smiling with pleasure, and know that they are there because in their own way they *too* love you, experience a sense of connectedness with you, and want to share their support for you and your life choices.

Experience their love and support, that of your extended family, your new in-laws, new siblings, new children, by simply creating the attitude that will help you cope with any potential crisis with the greatest of aplomb. Direct your thoughts to embrace the love you feel, and the joy that surrounds you, and your wedding will truly be the high point of your life that it *can* be.

At moments of potential tension, upset, or crisis, when something large or small is not just exactly the way you wanted it to be, remind yourself that the purpose of the ceremony is to unite you in marriage with the one you love. *That* will happen regardless of the frosting on the cake or the song the band plays as you walk down the aisle, and that is the true celebration of your love.

Part Three

THE
INTERFAITH
MARRIAGE

Chapter IX

LIVING
WITH DIFFERENCES

"Couples in this situation are more cohesive. We *must* embrace each other, be honest, sincere, and sensitive to our mate, because we have only each other to rely on. We work at being very caring and sensitive to each other all the time. We try harder to work out any problems together."

—Ruth, forty-two, interfaith married ten years

Donald and Karen must have had this same argument at least fifty times in the past two years of their marriage, but it seemed as if they never grew tired of it. "I don't understand how you can stand that music," Donald would say, as he walked into the room shaking his head. "If it isn't The Police, it's Springsteen or The Cars. I'll just never understand your taste. You'd think we grew up in different generations."

"*My* taste in music!" Karen would counter. "You must have been born thirty years behind your time. If it isn't 'mellow' or classical, you think it isn't music at all. What happened to your youth? Did rock and roll pass you by while you were studying for college exams or something?"

This would continue until they both laughed at the musical "narrow-mindedness" of the other and agreed not to play their own music unless they were alone or wore headphones.

As you might imagine, the differences in Donald and Karen's musical tastes did not prove to be a significant barrier to a loving, supportive relationship between them, and their marriage thrived as they searched together for as many areas of *common* interest to share as they could.

Working out differences of all kinds, from the foods you like to eat, the number of times you like to eat in a restaurant each week versus the number of meals cooked at home, to whether you want to finance a car or pay cash for it, is part and parcel of developing any successful marriage.

There will never be another you in the history of the universe. There will never be *anyone* else with your particular combination of genes and chromosomes, your particular social background, your life experiences, your attitudes, your dreams, your fantasies, your thoughts, your habits, your likes and dislikes, your unique mixture of nurture and nature.

Your task in life is simply to be the very best *you* that you can, for you are the only one who will ever have that opportunity and that challenge. Since each of us is unique, it stands to reason that no two people will have exactly the same needs, desires, interests, tastes, or outlook on the world, either. It should be obvious then that life in a relationship is of necessity a constant give and take, a perpetual negotiation between your needs and your partner's on a hundred different levels and issues.

Just as every day couples are able to work out their differences in other areas, so too they have successfully negotiated their religious needs in ways that have created harmony, peace, a sense of mutual respect, and a commitment to the emotional and spiritual well-being of each partner in the marriage as well.

As with every aspect of your relationship, I believe that what is most needed is to develop what I call the team marriage. In a team marriage, both partners treat each other as an integral and essential aspect of their own life. Each member of the team knows that it is his/her role to give 100% support to the other.

The team marriage approach is simply a way of realizing that you are in this life and marriage *together*. You need each other to provide a safe and secure environment in which to take risks with each other and stretch your horizons to include the experiences and background of the other and incorporate them into your own life. This way the interfaith aspect of your marriage can become an enriching element rather than a divisive one.

In the team marriage you face the world with a partner. You know that you are never alone because the two of you are committed to meeting each experience, each potential obstacle, as yet another opportunity to express that partnership. Team marriages grow out of a desire to create something that sets the two of you apart from other people and other relationships.

A good example of how the team marriage concept works in real life can be seen in the relationship of Eddie and Heather, whom we met earlier. Although there was a considerable amount of tension emanating from Eddie's parents before the actual wedding took place, they all did their best to get along *after* the ceremony, which is a fairly typical family response.

Eddie and Heather have developed an ongoing communication strategy that forms an integral part of their very successful interfaith marriage. Their way of approaching each potential problem within the relationship is a perfect example of how the team marriage works in a practical, concrete fashion.

"She'd never been exposed to a Jewish mother before!" Eddie laughed. "In her upbringing there wasn't that sense of closeness that we experience, and she wasn't sure how to handle it at first."

"Yes, I felt for a long time like 'How am I ever going to get *in* there?' I felt like an outsider. But once I did get in and was accepted as part of the family, it really felt great. In truth, Eddie helped me a lot in this process by explaining that it wasn't something personal with me but simply his family's way of doing things, and so he'd help me to integrate into this new environment."

"I'd help articulate the differences in our backgrounds as well as I could see them, and try to feel how *she* might be feeling, or how *she* might be seeing a particular ritual, event, or moment with my family," Eddie said. "I think that helped create a sense of togetherness in our relationship, for she knew that we were really in this together, all the way. It made us both feel more connected and secure in our partnership."

"That was the best part for me," Heather confessed. "He was always by my side every step of the way, and was trying his best to be helpful and sympathetic to my feelings. Just knowing that he was consciously trying all the time made it easier to not be as bothered by little things that otherwise might have upset me."

With Eddie and Heather the team approach had developed naturally out of their intense caring for the feelings of the other. They recognized that they came from different backgrounds, that they had different expectations of family roles and behavior as a result of these differences, and that they needed each other to be tolerant and respectful of how each had been raised when it came to family life-style and their relationship with in-laws.

"She'd ask, 'Why is your mom always prying into our affairs?' and I'd explain that it is simply part of the close family life that we have always shared among ourselves. It is just a way of being involved and showing that you care about what your kids are doing and what is going on in their lives. It was, however, a difference in upbringing and life-style between us that we had to grow to understand."

This team marriage approach worked so well with Eddie and Heather that it helped them develop a sense of humor about their own misperceptions as well. They were constantly sharing with each other ways in which they had misunderstood the intentions of an in-law as a result of simple ignorance of family customs and life-style.

Eddie commented, "Sometimes we stereotype other people's beliefs and backgrounds. It happens all around us in the world, and it happens in interfaith marriages as well. For example, something will happen where my mother will call us two or three times in one day to find out about a particular thing that is going on, or to tell us something, and Heather will remark, "Your typical Jewish mother again with her nose in everything." Depending upon whether or not you have a loving, supportive, and caring relationship, that kind of remark will either produce a chuckle on the Jewish partner's part, or be seen as hurtful and resented. With us, it gets a laugh."

As you can see, in a team marriage there is an underlying foundation of absolute trust in your partner. In interfaith marriages, even more than in same-faith, this kind of approach is crucial since not only does it give you the sense of security and support that is so important in any marriage, it allows you the freedom to ask questions and challenge the way your partner and his/her family do things, knowing that your partner will know that what you do and say is meant to be equally supportive and nurturing of him/her.

You can identify a team marriage by the way in which the individual partners characterize their relationship. For example, when Bill and Monica described the way in which they approach their relationship, they told me, "We don't hide things from each other and we know that it is totally up to us to create a relationship that is based on honesty. After all, if we aren't totally honest with each other it will only eventually hurt us and our relationship. Trust is the essential component."

Fran and Michael described their attitude in even simpler terms. "It's *our* family, *our* marriage, *our* home, and *our* children and we stick together on issues with the outside."

In the best relationships there are both the recognition that differences in background do exist and the ability to create an attitude of mutual respect, tolerance, and cooperation. Such relationships also show a willingness by both parties to sit down to explore rationally *together* the potential impact that these differences might have on the marriage.

This allows the couple to develop clear support strategies between them, aimed at helping each other to understand and live with these differences in ways that add luster and quality to their lives. Strategies that I have seen developed include the following:

1. Whenever an argument erupts over a difference in background, one party or the other calls "time," and both sit down and write out their feelings and the source of their disagreement. They then exchange writings, and by the time they finish reading and commenting on them, they inevitably have cooled down enough to work out a compromise.

2. At a time when things are going well and there are no outstanding quarrels or disagreements between them, the couple agrees upon a plan whereby they alternate in decision-making roles regarding religious differences. "This holiday you decide, and the next one I decide."

3. Both partners agree in advance *never* to allow parents to

come between them or put them in a position where they have to choose between a parent and a spouse when it comes to religious issues (or any other issue for that matter!).

4. Both partners agree to take an Introduction to _____ (Judaism, Catholicism, etc.) class together to learn more about each other's background.

5. Partners may agree in writing prior to a marriage ceremony exactly which holidays they will celebrate and how. This agreement may be subject to review annually, or at any length of time the couple may agree upon.

6. In some relationships, when an issue arises that appears to be the result of differences in background or upbringing, each partner speaks to the other's parents to get a better picture of how they were raised and which life experiences might have produced this particular feeling or point of view.

7. If at first you don't succeed, talk, talk, talk, talk, talk, talk, talk, talk, talk, talk, until you do.

Perhaps one of the most important things that you can learn from this chapter is that there *are* differences between members of interfaith marriages (and we'll see some of them in a moment). Acknowledging that these differences exist can be a liberating *and* binding experience for both partners. Such acknowledgment is a necessary prerequisite to any successful and supportive team marriage.

If you have chosen to be a part of an interfaith marriage, first admit that the differences are there. Only after you are honest about the differences themselves can you create a way together to transcend those differences and continue supporting each other in your ongoing quest to build a strong, enduring, loving marriage.

Differences as Gifts

Differences are not necessarily barriers in a relationship. Differences can be, in fact, *opportunities* for mutual support and decision making. Each issue, whether it is finances or the celebration of religious holidays, is an opportunity to reinforce the love and caring that form the foundation of your relationship. In fact, the way in which you successfully resolve areas of disagreement is one of the single best indicators of the resiliency and inner strength of your relationship itself.

Confronting the differences in the one you love is a difficult task for many people, but one that is crucial to the success of your marriage. Pretending that these differences don't exist or that they aren't really important, and that they will somehow take care of themselves, is a self-deception certain to bring frustration and unhappiness in the end. Frustration delayed is not frustration avoided. If it is left to build up inside for too long, when it finally does emerge (as it inevitably will) it will be blown all out of proportion and become much more destructive to the well-being of the relationship than it might otherwise have been.

Some of the differences between you are significant, perhaps most of them are not. Either way, it is crucial for you to plumb the depths of those differences, share your feelings with each other, your religious expectations and needs, your dreams and mental pictures of how the future will be for you and your potential children together, and discover which are serious and which are trivial for you.

The challenge of an interfaith marriage is to create harmony out of differences, mutual respect and love in the midst of ambiguity and paradox. See every difference as a gift from your partner's past, a window into a world that you have never known. Each difference that you uncover is yet another example of something that you can learn about and from each other, to add a unique and special dimension to your relationship and your love.

Learning from Each Other

Seeing differences as opportunities and gifts, rather than as barriers and liabilities, is another way of suggesting that you do your best to turn the apparent negatives of interfaith marriage into positives.

For example, consider every difference between you as an opportunity for learning and growth. An interfaith relationship provides the perfect opportunity to be engaged in such a process.

See your life as an ongoing laboratory of religious, spiritual, and ritual exploration. Be eager both to share your own background and religious upbringing with your partner, and to learn of a whole new world of practice and belief from him/her as well.

"The essential point is not whether the couple agrees on every issue of religion," Michelle (thirty-seven, Jewish, married to Andy, thirty-eight, a Congregationalist, for six years) told me. "It is rather their ability to discuss these issues in the proper supportive manner. We met at an assertiveness training class and use those techniques with each other all the time."

"I believe that *any* communication skills development will help an interfaith relationship," Andy added. "There *has* to be openness and a willingness to compromise within every relationship. After all, especially for an interfaith relationship to work, you have to be willing to not always be right, and *that* is hard for a lot of people, especially men."

Approaching your relationship as an opportunity for learning and growth at every turn is probably one of the most positive and healthy approaches that you could take in an interfaith marriage. Learn to see each day as an adventure, as a chance to discover something new and unique about your partner, yourself, or your relationship, and you will help ensure that the "magic" never departs.

There are often lessons to be learned within an interfaith marriage that were never contemplated by either partner in advance. Take Aron and Deidre, for example.

When I spoke with them a little over a year after their wedding, Deidre expressed surprise and a touch of amazement at the kind of lessons she felt she had learned in that relatively short time with Aron.

"Being married to a Jewish person has been an eye-opening experience for me," she said. "I have grown more sensitive and aware of the feelings of the Jews as a people, their concerns regarding anti-Semitism and the prejudice in the world around us, than I ever would have had I not married Aron. It has added a new dimension to my life and my perceptions of the world in which we live. *That* is a bonus that I simply never expected, which only came because *I* was willing to learn from the interfaith nature of the relationship."

Yes, the openness to learning from an interfaith marriage can make the difference between frustration over the things that divide you from the one you love, and excitement at the possibility of all that you can share with and learn from each other.

The Mind-Reading Syndrome

The single most destructive attribute that I have seen among the couples who come to me for counseling is what I call the mind reading syndrome. This ubiquitous problem strikes couples of all ages, from newlyweds to those married for decades, and I believe it is responsible for more marital disharmony than any other single relationship phenomenon.

It works like this. Jerry and Lori are sitting at home one evening watching television. Jerry just had a day filled with complaints from his boss, problems with his secretary, and work that seemed to pile up with each passing hour, and to top off the end of the day, his car got a flat tire on the way home. All he wants to do now is stare blankly at the TV screen, hoping that it will lull him into semiconsciousness, and as soon as humanly possible he will slip into bed with the hope that the morning will bring a better day, and a brighter emotional outlook on life.

Lori had a wonderful day at *her* office. A project she completed got rave reviews from her boss and colleagues, an article that she has written may be published in the company paper; and a friend she adores but hasn't seen for months dropped in unexpectedly for lunch. She is excited, stimulated by the day's events, and sits in front of the TV thinking about how much she'd like to be held and stroked by her husband.

This situation is duplicated nightly in millions of households. The catch is, of course, that being a typical couple, they keep their thoughts to themselves, and simply *wait* for their spouse to do the "right" thing to satisfy their needs of the moment.

Jerry sits waiting for Lori to mercifully suggest that they turn in for the night, while Lori sits waiting for Jerry to move closer on the couch so she can snuggle up. Neither says anything about their feelings to the other. The usual scenario will find Jerry eventually saying, "I'm tired, let's go get some sleep," and Lori, who is then somewhat put off and upset by his disconnected and unromantic response to the situation, tightens her jaw, sighs, and answers, "Fine."

Now I know that when I describe it this way, it sounds *a bit* silly and *a bit* childish. It seems so obvious that if one or the other of them would just open their mouths and *tell* their partner how they are feeling and what they want and need, they could work it out so that at least one if not both of them will be satisfied. Either way, there would be no lingering resentment over needs unfulfilled, or the supposition that one partner just wasn't caring enough or tuned in enough to the other.

Time and time again I hear someone say, "She ought to know what I want," or "He should just know by now what I need." Forget it! Try as we might, none of us are mind readers. Oh, yes, from time to time I finish a sentence that my wife started, or say something only to hear her exclaim, "I was just thinking that exact thing!" and we smile and feel that warm sense of togetherness and connectedness that comes from being close and in love with someone wonderful.

That, however, is a far cry from believing that I can read her mind and will know when she needs to be held and stroked, left alone with her own thoughts, or listened to while she tells me of the remarkable events of her day. From one moment to the next she may need any and all of the above, and the only way I'll know which it is, is if *she tells me*. The truth is that most of the time you *do* want to give your partner what it is that will make them happy, and they want to do the same for you. Most of the time your partner would *love* to give you what you want and need, and would be thrilled beyond belief to have a direct pipeline to that important information. The good news is that there is a ridiculously simple solution to this dilemma, one that will immediately help. *Tell them!*

Imagine how much simpler life would be if your spouse *told* you every time he or she wanted to be held or kissed or listened to or talked to. Imagine if you could count on the fact that 100% of the time, if they needed or wanted something from you, they would ask. Think of how relieved you would be, how much weight would lift from your shoulders, how much easier and simpler your relationship would be.

It *can* be that way all the time, but *you* must be the one to make it so. Interfaith marriages have enough stresses and tensions built in that they don't need any more created by the participants themselves. Misunderstandings and frustrations are a result of poor communication most of the time, and fixing that is both the simplest and hardest thing on earth. Simplest because all it takes is opening your mouth and telling your partner what you need and want all the time. Hardest because our egos and sense of self are often so fragile that our fear of rejection is stronger than our need to insure that we get what we want.

This is often what keeps us from doing what makes sense, namely, *asking*. Remember, if you don't ask for what you want and need in life, there is a good chance that you won't get it. If you do ask for what you want, you are increasing your chances a hundredfold that your life will be filled with satisfaction and joy.

The Many Forms That Differences Take

"When we first started dating it was all so exciting and wonderful that it never occurred to me we were different at all," Florence confessed. "I guess I was a bit naive at the time, but I just thought things would continue along in the blissful way that they had started. I thought that any differences would melt away like snow in the spring. It's funny how being excited and in love allows you to ignore things that your otherwise rational mind would tell you might just be important some day."

"Yes," Arthur responded, "I felt the same way at first. Like, so what if she's Jewish and I'm Catholic; so what if our parents are different, if we were raised differently. We didn't *seem* very different. You know there is basically very little difference in the way we live, the values we have, the things that we like to do. The other stuff, like Christmas and Hanukkah, Passover and Easter, isn't really very important.

"Of course when we started really getting serious about our relationship, all of a sudden certain things became increasingly important. Like, for example, it never occurred to me that my child wouldn't be baptized. In fact it seemed so natural and obvious to me that I never even brought it up. Only when Florence's mother mentioned something one day about having a baby naming or a bris with her favorite rabbi whenever we have kids did I realize, 'Hey, there just might be a difference in expectations here that we'd better talk about.'"

"That was really the first major religious argument we had," Florence said. "I realized that he expected that *my* child would be baptized, and I said, 'No way that is happening to any child of mine.' All of a sudden we began to discover a few hidden, rather strong emotional attachments that each of us had to our own religious background without even being aware of it.

"Religion is a funny thing. You don't seem to use it until you need it. It's something that you take for granted, and most of the time something you rebel against or argue about with your parents.

"Then out of the blue you get hit with a religion attack as you are about to get married to someone. Things that weren't important before all of a sudden become very important to you and sometimes you don't even know why."

Florence and Arthur are an excellent example of what I discovered in many interfaith relationships. Uncovering one's *true* religious feelings, the differences that do exist within couples, often takes *time* to happen. For many, this realization develops slowly over the years of their relationship. In fact, I have heard observers of interfaith marriages comment on the apparent "delayed reaction" that seemed to take place in one individual or another who "suddenly" had a personal religious revelation and discovered that they really *did* care about their religious background after all.

Such revelations are not uncommon and in my experience stem mostly from the confrontation between an individual and a specific life-cycle event or series of events in which they are or would like to be involved. For example, Florence and Arthur have a perfectly compatible relationship where religious issues are not a problem, *until* Arthur is confronted with a normal life event that calls forth a perfectly natural religiously based emotional response—namely, "When my child is born I feel a need to have him/her baptized."

For some, it takes a series of events over time to evoke a strong enough emotional reaction to suddenly plunge the individual, and, as a matter of course, the couple into a religious crisis. Perhaps it has been the participation in a dozen Christmas dinners with the in-laws, with the tree brightly lit in the background, which finally pushes the Jewish partner's consciousness over the edge of the comfort zone to produce a feeling of religious betrayal and abandonment.

I have spoken to many couples who are struggling with defining the differences between them, and searching for the specific strategies that will allow them to have their respective religious needs met. Often they have told me that it took experiences such as those I have just shared to bring their "true" feelings to the surface.

They are usually much harder on themselves than they ought to be. The reality is that our "true" feelings *change* over time, along with, it is to be hoped, the rest of us. Change is one of the few constants in life, and interfaith marriages are not free from the inevitability of its impact.

Arthur's true feelings may have been one thing when he and Florence were dating and first married, and legitimately something quite different when their first child was born. That is the way real human beings live in this imperfect world of ours, and it is important and helpful to your own peace of mind to accept it in yourself and your partner.

Part of the difficulty in making promises to each other in an interfaith marriage is the knowledge that we do in fact change over time. What is unimportant today may become very important tomorrow, and what is desperately important today becomes something we smile at in disbelief ten years from now.

Discovering your own religious feelings is an ongoing process that involves honesty with yourself and your partner, the willingness to acknowledge that your feelings are legitimate whatever they may be, and the recognition that yesterday's feelings may not be today's. Only by honestly confronting these feelings can you successfully structure a loving interfaith relationship that will allow for different needs and emotional/spiritual paths to fulfillment and satisfaction.

Many of the couples with whom I spoke admitted readily that they recognized a number of differences between them as a result of being raised in different religions. These differences were expressed in attitudes and expectations, in life-style choices and child-raising decisions, as well as other subtle and not so subtle ways that they could identify.

"The only difference I see is in attitudes about birth control," Monica told me. "A child is a child at the moment of conception for Catholics, and I know that for Jews a child is a child only at birth. I had an abortion once and it was hard for me to deal with, coming from my Catholic background. I felt terribly guilty for a very long time, but I finally dealt with it.

"Bill was a big help, especially because he helped me to see that there are other ways of looking at the world, other ways of thinking about birth, life, and the essence of creation than the traditional Catholic way that I was taught. I think if I had married a Catholic, I probably would have ended up with more kids, even though I really didn't want any more.

"Money issues are different too. I was taught not to think that money was okay—to spend it only on the children but not on yourself, ever. Bill handles money better and sees it in its proper perspective. Money isn't bad or evil as with my religion. Sin is connected to it in Catholicism and not in Judaism.

"Bill also doesn't seem to have any need to confess, which is something that I want to do all the time. Now, since I no longer go to church to confessional, I 'confess' at the smallest things just with friends and family. He takes things a lot more lightly than I do. Sins are viewed differently with Jews, not so serious, not so heavy at all."

Monica sat thinking back over her life together with Bill, and then came up with yet another clear difference that grew directly out of their respective religious backgrounds. "I respect the intellectual nature of Judaism—the fact that it is a rational religion that doesn't demand that you give blind obedience to unbelievable things. You can discuss issues on an intellectual level, even when emotion is a part of it, which it inevitably is with religion. I think that is one of the biggest differences in our religious upbringing."

The issues of money and intellectualism among Jews are common themes in the perceived differences according to the couples with whom I spoke.

For example, in thinking back over the beginnings of her relationship with Jack, Diane recalled, "The first difference showed up when we first met. His perception was that all Jews were rich, and so I kept trying to show him that he was wrong. His mom had that impression too, so whenever I went to his house I would show up in jeans and a t-shirt just to demonstrate that I wasn't rich!

"Actually, I see a lot of differences between us, but I'm not always sure that I can identify exactly what they are. It's sort of an outlook on life, an attitude that just seems Jewish or non-Jewish."

"I know what she means," Jack added with a shake of his head. "We know other interfaith couples and they all seem to share the same opinion—that there *are* differences. Even such simple things as the fact that Jews like to dine out. For them, it's like an 'experience,' and all I want to do is just gobble it down and go do something else."

Diane thought of another major area of difference. "Savings and money are a lot different too. I do put away money, but if it were up to me we'd spend it on what we want. He tends to do more saving. We pay bills differently too. Jack says pay the bills first and play with what's left and I do the opposite. I just figure the bills will wait until *I* get around to them."

"I call her my little Manischewitz," Jack chuckled, "because she 'whines' all the time!" He laughed and so did she as he added, just in case I thought he was serious, "It's a joke, and if she ever was offended by it, I would never say it again."

Diane continued, "I remember that the differences in our religious background really hit me one day before we were married. I wondered if Jack could give me the kind of life-style I wanted and was used to. Just after we got engaged, I suddenly realized that some of his attitudes were really different from the way I was raised, and I wondered if he would be able to give me all the advantages that I grew up with.

"I saw my father as a typical Jewish father, who worked hard all the time to make a home for us. I don't know if it's because we're Jewish or not, but I am and was spoiled by him. It was a big shock and change when he said, 'Now you're on your own.' Just giving up the credit cards and all that freedom to spend was hard for me. That was a part of my life-style that I'd grown used to. But, I'd rather have the happiness of our relationship than all the credit cards in the world."

Jack was smiling during all of this. After a few moments he

chuckled as he thought of one more difference between his background and Diane's. "Her parents think I'm the most handy guy in the world. Why? Because I fix things and don't call a repairman the minute something doesn't work. She's always saying, 'Let's just pick up the phone and call someone.' I don't know if it has anything to do with being Jewish, or it's just her family, but it sure is different from the way *I* was raised."

Some people see differences as barriers and will do whatever is necessary to remove them from the relationship. Richard and Lisa are one such couple. Though raised in a relatively traditional Jewish home, Richard sees the differences, as compared with the similarities, between Christians and Jews as so minor that it isn't worth the price you have to pay to stay different. He didn't want his children to have to experience the potential suffering of being a minority within a majority culture.

"Homogeneity is just easier," he told me, "whether with two cultures or two religions. The main positive that I got from Judaism is that we are the 'People of The Book,' with an importance placed on education for both economic stability and the opportunity to develop your mind. I lost my ceremonial relationship with Judaism long ago, so giving up Jewish holidays and celebrations is really no loss for me at all."

Though some would argue with or perhaps even be offended by, Richard's personal decision to abandon his own Jewish background in favor of what he considered to be "mainstream American religious culture," he *has* taken control of his life. His attitude has created a positive, nurturing, and supportive relationship, and it is one of the possible and not infrequently used methods of coping with the potential stress of interfaith differences.

One of the most sensitive areas of difference within an interfaith marriage concerns the emotional power of religious symbols. Religion is one of those areas of life that tend to be loaded with emotional buttons that most of us don't even know are there, until something someone does or says pushes one of our buttons and sends us reeling.

Simply recognizing that differences exist in our religious background is not enough to curb the often irrational and unexpected emotional reactions to religion and religious symbols. These emotions often lie hidden deeply beneath the years of life's experiences that have dulled their sharpness and buried them out of sight and feeling.

As we have seen in many of the relationships in this chapter, it often takes a specific religious occasion or celebration, life-cycle event, or moment of stress to unearth these deep-seated religious feelings. Often they appear at holiday times, when emotions tend to run high anyway.

Without a doubt, Christmas and Hanukkah create the most concrete examples of emotional disharmony as a result of religious upbringing. One typical interfaith response was that of John and Melony. Each year saw an ongoing struggle between them to reach a Hanukkah/Christmas compromise, and each year the conflict seemed to focus around the external symbols of the holidays.

"We have one of those situations where nobody gets totally what they want," John said. "I'm not comfortable putting a menorah in the window of our home during Hanukkah, and her family isn't comfortable with a Christmas tree in our living room. Most of the time we don't have one, and when we do we call it a Hanukkah bush. I don't feel strongly about it, actually, though I'd like a wreath on the door. Her father made some comments about it when I did put one up, so we took it off."

I was unhappy with the wreath at the time as well," Melony added. "It offended my family and made me uncomfortable. I guess now it would be okay to put one up, but without lights. I don't like the wreath; it symbolizes a Christian home and I'm uncomfortable with that aspect. But we never fight about religion."

As you can see, religious symbols *are* often carriers of deep religious emotion. For Melony, the wreath with lights on the door was a symbol of a "Christian" home. Her negative reaction to the wreath was based totally upon her personal, emotional interpretation of its significance, the wreath providing an excellent focal point for the discovery and expression of her own religious feelings.

For John, the tree, the wreath, and the decorations for Christmas were symbols of his belief in Jesus as the Messiah and Son of

God. His emotional reaction to the absence of these symbols in his home, although painful for him personally and stressful for them as a couple, provided them the opportunity to share their feelings openly and honestly.

One of the best strategies for coping with these religious differences is to ask your partner to help you experience life and see the world through *their* eyes and *their* perspective.

The ability to see the world through another's eyes is indeed one of the most important relationship skills that a couple can learn. Every interfaith relationship is filled with numerous opportunities for misunderstanding. Couples raised in different religious communities have different understandings of the meaning and symbolism in religious words, activities, prayers, songs, rituals, and physical objects.

Jews and Christians, for example, each react very differently to a cross. A cross clearly has nothing to do with right and wrong, but reactions to it are the natural outgrowth of an upbringing in one faith community or another that *attaches* given meanings and associations to the cross. For a Christian, it may be that looking at the cross evokes warm memories of quiet family gatherings on Christmas or Easter, the inspirational music of a church choir, the salvation of the world to come, or the love of Jesus for humanity. For a Jew, depending upon his or her upbringing and life experiences, that same cross may represent cossacks looting and killing Jews in Czarist Russia, the Crusaders burning Jews on their way to the Holy Land, or the church-sponsored Inquisition in Spain forcibly converting Jews to Christianity with torture and the threat of death.

It is the responsibility of *both* partners to provide the other with the *tools* to understand their world view. It doesn't just happen automatically because you love someone.

It is difficult for us to realize, or to acknowledge even to ourselves, that we have a specific outlook on life, a particular way of looking at the world that may not always be shared by others, including those we love. It is even harder to admit that the world view of another isn't always "wrong" simply because it is different.

The ability to acknowledge the "otherness" of another, without automatically labeling that otherness as "wrong," is one of the major marks of maturity in relationships. Business partnerships fall apart daily because one partner is constantly imposing *his* or *her* view on the other, constantly making judgments that the other is wrong, even when it is merely a different point of view.

It is even more crucial in a love relationship to develop the self-control and inner strength of character to resist the snap judgments, the automatic put-downs, the instant disapproval of your partner's opinion when it differs from yours. It is an essential element of a successful interfaith marriage for both partners to exhibit enough respect for the other's opinions, intelligence, and sensitivity to allow for differences in points of view.

Think back over the length of any relationship that you have been involved with. Inevitably there were moments of disagreement between you and your partner. Inevitably there were times when you argued over an issue, perhaps even passionately, believing that *you* were right and the other wrong. If you are honest with yourself, you will probably admit that in many of these instances it was *not* really an issue of right and wrong at all.

Most of the disagreements that couples experience are less issues of substance, and more issues of style, life-style, personal taste, or individual choice. Most of the time couples argue over issues that are a matter of personal predilection, individual point of view, and *not* issues of "objective" fact. It therefore stands to reason that in most of these instances of disagreement there *is* no right and wrong in the absolute sense.

How many marital or relationship disputes would *never* take place at all if the individuals involved were able to step back from the heat of the moment, suspend their own judgments and positions on a given matter, and try to see the world from their partner's point of view? I believe from my own experience in counseling and speaking with hundreds of people that *most* relationship disagreements could be avoided in this way.

Be open with your partner and remember that they are seeing the world *not* through your life experiences, but through theirs. Often in my own life, in the midst of feeling frustrated or angry at the way someone else has reacted to a given situation, I have found myself saying, "I bet if *I* had grown up with their life experiences, if *I* had gone through everything that they have gone through in their lives, had the parents they had, the friends they had, the teachers they had, I bet that *I* would react *exactly the same way."*

It's amazing what little effort it takes to allow your judgmental mind to rest for a moment, long enough to take an objective look at the situation and realize that *if you were them,* you would feel the same way, too. Once that happens, there is an automatic relaxation of tension in the relationship, for you no longer have two "sides" struggling to do things *their* way, fighting for emotional validation of *their* point of view and indirectly their sense of self-worth as well.

Religion as the Scapegoat

One of the most potentially destructive phenomena that occurs in many interfaith families involves the identification of normal, everyday marital tensions or pre-wedding stresses with the "interfaith" nature of the marriage.

When a couple is involved in an interfaith relationship, they often discover that others have many preconceived stereotypes about the "problems" that they will "inevitably" experience as a result of their different religious backgrounds. All too often, I have seen parents of interfaith couples pounce upon an individual incident of pre-wedding-planning tension and declare, "You see, I knew there would be problems in an interfaith marriage."

This is usually followed by some version of "I told you so," or perhaps "I knew this would happen if you married a _____." (Fill in the blank with your partner's religion.)

The area of tension may simply be one of a dozen average, run-of-the-mill, garden-variety, totally understandable and predictable stress points that happen in *every* marriage, or are a part of *every* pre-wedding experience. Allowing family and friends to use *their* stereotypes to blame your partner's religion or ethnic group for this normal stress can be very destructive to your relationship.

There can be tension over who is to be invited, where people are to be seated, the menu, the minister/rabbi, the color of the attendants' dresses, and a hundred other possible issues that have to be kept in their proper perspective. They are *not* necessarily related to your religious differences, and when everything is lumped together under that great generalization, you may end up suffering needlessly from despair and doubt.

Diane, the Jewish partner in an interfaith marriage, acknowledged this experience in her own marriage when she told me, "Yes, 'religious' tensions appear mostly because they seem to be an easy and convenient issue on which to focus. Someone will say, 'It's because she's Jewish,' or 'It's natural since he's Christian,' even when that doesn't have anything whatsoever to do with a given issue or situation." Once again, stereotypes of others, and of interfaith marriage itself, take on a destructive power all their own.

Monica shared with me a conviction expressed by many who are involved with interfaith marriages when she said, "If a marriage will fall apart, it will do so anyway, and religion becomes just an excuse for the problems that otherwise exist. Religion is just the way you are; it's not something to be used against someone you love."

By now it must be clear that what is necessary to ensure that you will create a mature, mutually loving, and nourishing relationship is that you *take responsibility for all your choices*. Give up the easy way out, of blaming others and the circumstances of your life for the decisions that you have freely made. That is one of the single most important steps you can take on the road to a successful marriage, a happy, joy-filled life, and the peace of mind that comes from knowing your life is turning out the way you really want it to.

Think about it for a moment. The reality is, your life *is* turning out the way you want it to. You have made the choices that have led you to the life you now lead.

Now that you are involved with or married to someone of another religious background, your life has the possibility of even more diverse experiences, even more growth and expansion as you soak up your partner's background, ideals, dreams, rituals, history, and family. It can either be a disaster or an exciting adventure for you, *if* you see it that way.

One of the major advantages to taking complete responsibility for your life is that you and your partner can discuss issues and potential problems on an equal footing. When one of you assumes the passive, dependent role within the relationship, it makes it much harder to have open and honest discussions about anything important.

Both partners have to be willing to choose freely that which they want out of life. Both must be willing to say, "This is what I need, this is what I am willing to give, this is what I feel comfortable with, and this is what I feel uncomfortable with." This is especially important when it comes to the sensitive area of religion and religious observance and rituals.

So relax and enjoy the life you have created and be willing to say to yourself, "Look at all the wonderful things I *do* have in my life. Look at the friends I have made, the experiences I have shared, the things I have done, and the growth and learning I have accomplished." Take pride in who you are, and in the fact that you have a lifetime ahead to continue this process of growth and discovery.

Chapter X

CREATING YOUR
OWN RELIGIOUS LIFE-STYLE

"Any couple in an interfaith marriage needs
to establish what is important to *them*
together. They need to set goals and priorities
and then guide their life accordingly."

—Judy, interfaith married fifteen years

Lee and Rickie had been married almost a year before they had
their first blowup over religion. It began as so many do with a
simple, innocent comment.

As Lee told it to me, he had been watching a talk show on
television where the subject of the separation of church and state
was being discussed. One of the guests on the show was arguing
strongly that Christmas programs in school were a natural expression of the religion of the founding fathers and represented the
"spiritual foundation of our country."

As he continued to listen to the discussion that ensued, he
turned to Rickie and said, "I'm always amazed at how passionate
people get over religion. I don't think religion of *any* kind should
be brought into public schools."

What ensued turned out to be an enlightening turning point in
their brief married life together. Rickie looked up with surprise
and replied, "That's interesting, because for me participating in

the annual Christmas play was the most memorable part of my entire childhood school experience."

Lee then responded that as far as *he* was concerned, bringing Christmas into the public school was an insult to non-Christians, an affront to their religious sensitivities, and a violation of the Constitution to boot.

Rickie shot back that she had always been proud that America was a Christian country, proud that the Pilgrims were good, charitable Christians, and proud of how tolerant America (meaning Christian America) had always been of foreigners (meaning non-Christians).

By this time the volume in the room had risen considerably, and Lee and Rickie found themselves in the middle of an all-out shouting match over the question of whether America was a "Christian" country or not, who was being tolerant of whom when it came to religion, and whether or not Jesus had any place within the halls of the local elementary school.

They quickly discovered that they both had deeper feelings about religion than they had previously thought. They also realized that there were things that they obviously hadn't ever talked about that might have an important bearing on decisions they would make regarding the kind of religious life they would create together.

One of the most important lessons that an interfaith couple can learn is the importance of sharing their true religious needs with one another. Part of the problem that inevitably faces interfaith couples is that they don't always *know* what their true religious needs are so as to be able to share them in the first place.

Back in Chapter IV we discussed the importance of discussing religion and child raising prior to the actual wedding ceremony. We also shared the experiences of many interfaith couples and how very often your needs and desires change over time as you grow and mature in life. What is irrelevant at age 23 may become vitally important at age 35. Often there is little that you can do to plan for these changes, beyond acknowledging that they will probably happen and keeping yourself as open as possible to the changes as they occur.

Regardless of your particular stage in life, particular life-style choices or personal religious beliefs, the crucial principle to accept for the health and welfare of your relationship is to share your needs with your partner. The argument between Lee and Rickie wasn't really about specific religious needs, but as a result of that particular discussion, they realized that there were probably *many* areas of personal religious belief, conviction, and need that they hadn't ever discussed with each other.

"We are probably like many interfaith couples," Rickie said. "We knew that religion was an area of disagreement and difference between us, so we stayed away from the subject as much as we could. Who wants to deliberately raise an issue that you know in advance will just cause friction, disagreement, and some form of upset between you and the person you love?"

"Exactly," Lee added. "I knew that my background, being raised Jewish in Detroit, was very different from Rickie's as a Southern Methodist from Georgia. I too stayed away from religious issues most of the time so as to keep our relationship focused on those areas of our lives that we do share, and that draw us together."

Both of them realized, as a result of the Christmas-in-the-school argument, that it was important for them to face up to the reality of their differences and see how to forge a mutual religious life-style together.

You can't hide for long from the truth, whether yours or your partner's. The best thing that you can do for your relationship is to acknowledge your true feelings and religious needs, share them with the one you love, and be willing to take the consequences. Whatever happens, when the relationship itself is a loving, caring, supportive one, you can approach each issue as a team, prepared to work out whatever will be best for the marriage, as well as for each other.

Let's look at some of the most common issues and problems that arise when couples are involved with creating their own religious life-style. Along with the problems, we will also see a number of successful strategies and ideas as to how you might best deal with this important lifelong issue in your relationship.

The Impulse to Recapture Nostalgia

Most of us grow up with some form of religious affiliation from early childhood. We experience a certain amount of ritual in our family life when we are children and come to unconsciously see whatever our *own* particular family did as simply the "right" way to do things religiously. We come to this decision in the "childhood" parts of our minds, without ever thinking about it or consciously making decisions on an adult level at all.

When we enter into a relationship with another adult, there are parts of our childhood memory that lie in wait to catch our "adult" minds off guard with their absolutism and certainty. I see this expressed most often in the conversations in my study between interfaith couples as they discuss their feelings about holidays and family celebrations.

Lee said, "I don't really care much about the holidays (meaning the High Holidays since he is Jewish; Christians use the same term to refer to Christmas and Easter), but I do have nice memories of them from my childhood." Rickie replied, "I don't really care either, but every Christmas when we don't have a tree it kind of bothers me."

The "kind of bothers me" part of the statement is her childhood memory calling out to be acknowledged and satisfied. The truth is she would be much happier if she celebrated Christmas each year with a tree, presents, lights, and the special dinner surrounded by family that she remembers from her youth. However, her adult mind thinks of it as an unnecessary aspect of the holiday that would probably only create some distance between her and her Jewish husband.

Since Rickie doesn't express her true feelings and religious needs, Lee is then unaware that she really *does* want to celebrate Christmas, and therefore isn't even given the chance to decide whether it is something he is willing to have in his home and relationship or not.

All of the above is a result of their poor communication skills, and of her unwillingness to acknowledge the below-the-surface emotional attachments she has to the religious symbols and rituals of her past. When asked to name the single most important factor in creating a successful, loving, and supportive interfaith relationship, five partners in interfaith marriages all pointed to the exact same thing:

LISA: "We talk a lot to each other, plain and simple."

MICHAEL: "We ask each other how we feel and talk it out till we find a solution to whatever the problem may be."

JUDY: "Ask and tell. That's it!"

MICHELLE: "Vigorous discussions about everything are the key. We talk about everything, since we both know that you can't read the other's mind."

MONICA: "We discovered that the most important aspect of our marriage is simply communication, open and honest communication. That was the key."

The key really is communication, and the challenge is to force yourself to share your feelings, dreams, needs, and emotions with your partner, *knowing* that they may feel totally the opposite, or simply not understand where you are coming from at all.

Worshiping as a Family

Throughout your life together as an interfaith family, you will be confronted with holidays, festivals, religious services, and family gatherings. Each time you will be forced to make choices as to what you will celebrate, when, and with whom.

Sometimes religious differences, although not a problem in the relationship, are still a source of some sadness and discontent. Walter, who is Southern Baptist, and Ruth, who is Jewish, have what appears to be a stable and mutually rewarding marriage relationship. Still, there are times when the religious differences that exist only serve to intensify the feelings of temporary distance between them.

Ruth shared her own misgivings about regular church attendance by pointing out how when she had gone to church, she kept hearing references to Jews that upset her. She went on, "The biggest issue between us is at Christmas time. Since we each follow our own religion in this household, when we have a tree I have mixed feelings about it. What is saddest to me is not worshiping as a family. It is either church or temple, and neither of us really feels totally comfortable in the other's religious environment."

Often when both members of the interfaith couple are desirous of attending a religious service that they would find meaningful, contemporary, and nonoffensive so that they might attend together, they end up at a Unitarian church. At times this solves the problem for both of them, since Unitarian services are often *not* based on traditional ideas of God as a supernatural being.

Within Judaism, Reconstructionism is also a nonsupernatural, rational, and intelligent contemporary approach to religious life that many interfaith couples find appealing. What attracts them to both Unitarianism and liberal forms of Judaism is that they are able to celebrate and worship together, without compromising their own backgrounds and beliefs.

Worshiping together is often a difficult experience, *not* because of the theological underpinnings of a particular religion or group, but simply because the services themselves are unfamiliar, and therefore uncomfortable.

A good example of the problem can be found in the marriage of Fran and Michael. Michael was Jewish; Fran had been raised Catholic and later converted to Judaism. Commenting upon the differences in their religions, Fran told me, "There is really a lot the same in the two religions, except of course belief in Jesus. In fact, mostly it was so similar that I kept wondering if I had missed something when I was learning about Judaism. It all seemed so comfortable for me."

Even so, it took a while for Fran to feel at home in a Jewish worship service, in spite of the fact that the religion itself was very comfortable for her. The beliefs were not a problem, it was the unfamiliarity with worship patterns, with liturgical music, with the content and style of Jewish worship as against the Catholic Mass, that took some time to adjust to.

Even more important, perhaps, is the *internal* expectation that both converts and non-Jewish partners in interfaith marriages have that they *will* feel uncomfortable before they even get to a Jewish service. Time and again I have been told, "I felt like when I got there everyone would be staring at me, pointing me out to each other and whispering that I didn't belong."

Such outward displays of rejection rarely if ever actually occur, but the *fear* of such an unpleasant and uncomfortable encounter is a normal reaction to feeling like an "outsider." This only serves to heighten the sense of otherness and being different that stands in the way of interfaith couples' creating a natural and mutually satisfying worship pattern.

"When I married Ruth," Walter said, "Baptists were very conservative so we looked for a middle ground of some kind, like the Unitarians or Presbyterians. What we eventually decided upon was an activist Presbyterian church. It was okay for a time, but I found it too cold and intellectual after what I had been raised with. I missed the emotion and up-tempo of my Southern Baptist upbringing.

"For a while we went to the temple, but then a split came because I couldn't totally embrace Judaism since I wasn't willing to let go of my belief in Jesus as the Messiah. Other than that, it was great.

"Jesus is really the main religious issue between us, and there is simply no solution to *that* problem. You either believe or you don't, and since it isn't really a 'rational' decision, you can't really argue about it. Since we love each other and want to stay together, we simply smooth over it and go on with our lives, each believing what we want."

This sense of frustration was expressed by many interfaith couples as we sat and discussed the choices and decisions that they have made in their religious lives. There is a sadness pervading many interfaith marriages that comes from the realization that one's beliefs are not something that can be given, taught, or imposed on someone who simply doesn't share them to begin with. Crossing that philosophical and religious chasm that separates so many is often itself purely an act of faith in its boldest manifestation.

Worshiping as a family can only take place if at least one of the partners in an interfaith team marriage is willing to push through the internal emotional barriers to participation in a religious service of another religion in a potentially strange and unfamiliar environment, with perhaps a foreign and unusual language thrown in to boot.

The act of choosing to transcend the emotional barriers that exist to a shared worship experience at times can become the ultimate test of your flexibility, support of each other, and tolerance of each other's background and beliefs.

"I'm saddened to know that Melony doesn't believe in Jesus," John said. "I believe very strongly, and sometimes I hide it. I'm sad that she doesn't have the same joy that I have, but I do believe that she'll go to heaven anyway as a good person with love in her heart for others."

Such theological pain that John suffers for the lack of belief in Jesus on the part of his wife Melony is typical of the lengths to which those involved with interfaith marriages will go to rationalize the acceptability of the one they love. There is a great gap looming between John and Melony that no amount of tolerance, no amount of hairsplitting, no amount of bending theology and belief will close.

There simply comes a point where the partners in an interfaith marriage must acknowledge that there are serious philosophical and emotional differences between them that are there to stay. There may never be a meeting of the minds, and their relationship may simply have to be one that doesn't include joint or family worship experiences together.

The Conspiracy of Silence

Richard and Lisa are a perfect example of yet another all too common phenomenon of interfaith relationships. They seemed to love everything there was about each other. They were constant companions, lived together for three years, and had what appeared to be a smooth, easygoing, and obviously fun relationship.

They had slipped into this relationship effortlessly after meeting at a party of a mutual friend and discovering that there was a physical attraction with sparks flying from the very start. In fact, they had such a lovely, tension-free relationship that they were willing to do almost *anything* to keep it that way, but the costs were higher than they imagined.

In order to keep their relationship exactly as they wanted it, they each had to live a life of silent deception. They were co-conspirators in an elaborate and unexpressed relationship game— a game that relied upon their total cooperation without their ever exchanging a single word about it. The game is called *Conspiracy of Silence*.

In the conspiracy of silence each partner is afraid of upsetting the relationship, and so they simply *say nothing* about their religious needs and feelings *at all*.

Each partner in the game ends up tiptoeing around any subject that remotely touches upon religion. Needs go unfulfilled, and desires go unexpressed. It is like planting a land mine in the midst of your favorite flower garden. It looks beautiful, but you have to walk so gingerly around each flower that the total concentration and effort required destroys the pleasure that you might have received from the viewing.

Like the land mine in the garden, the conspiracy of silence is deadly. It feeds on all the fears and insecurities that naturally haunt relationships anyway. Each of us is somewhat insecure, somewhat unsure of exactly what our partner is thinking and feeling all the time, and in interfaith relationships the opportunities for misunderstandings are endless.

Don't wait a minute longer to break down whatever walls of silence exist between you. Sharing your feelings, your dreams, and your fears with another is one of the most powerful ways there is to open *them* up to you. Try it and you will be amazed at how it works. When someone is willing to be vulnerable and open with us, it is practically impossible for *us* to remain closed with them.

The Willingness to Try

Creating your own religious life-style in an interfaith relationship is an exercise in patience, tolerance, flexibility, and self-control. It's easy to become frustrated when your partner doesn't understand why something that is important to you is important at all. It's easy to feel as if you are bumping up against a brick wall when the rituals that have warm and loving memories for you seem to represent embarrassment or intolerance or stir up childhood memories of prejudice and trauma for your mate.

One characteristic that appears to be invaluable to the emotional and spiritual health of interfaith relationships is simply the willingness to try different and new things. It will often pull you through potentially stress-filled decisions and agreements, and can create an environment in your relationship that allows for experimentation—trying things (such as holidays, rituals, celebrations) on for size to see how they feel to both of you.

There is something wonderful about an attitude of openness to new experiences and customs that allows you both to feel free to change your minds without feeling like one is "winning" and the other is "losing." It can be a liberating aspect of your interfaith relationship that prevents either of you from feeling defensive or protective about your own religion.

Cultivate and practice an attitude of experimentation, and you will feel that your life together is a constant source of new and exciting religious adventures. Try celebrating one way, and then try the same holiday a different way. First experiment with one holiday, and then try celebrating another. Throughout this process of trial and error, of *constant—perhaps lifelong*—experimentation, both you and your partner must be willing to monitor your feelings, determine whether you are comfortable or not, gauge how much meaning you are deriving from each holiday experience, and then *share* that information with each other.

Most interfaith couples do not have the intensity of belief in a particular religious dogma or system that would preclude some form of accommodation or compromise. If they did, they probably wouldn't have become involved with someone of another religion in the first place. Most, although certainly not all people who enter interfaith relationships, are part of the mainstream American religious experience, which includes an openness to other religions and a softening of sharp religious boundaries and barriers.

For many, the necessity to confront religious differences when it comes to holiday celebrations and rituals is seen as an opportunity for creative exploration, personal growth, and mutual cooperation and sharing. Eddie and Heather are just such a couple. Listen as they describe both the celebrations that they participate in, and the process through which they both feel personal growth and communal togetherness have been furthered.

"We celebrate all holidays and intermix families, and it works great," said Heather. "Of course, it helps a lot to have extended families that are supportive of us and what we want to do as well. After all, it would be a lot harder to do what we do if we got resistance from any of our parents. They seem to enjoy being a part of our various holiday celebrations, and each pair invites the other along with us to celebrate Passover, Christmas, Easter, Hanukkah, and other holiday times.

"When we celebrate Christmas, we do it more as a family celebration than as a 'religious holiday.' I might believe in my heart, inside, the theology that goes along with Christmas, but it's not something that we discuss or celebrate openly at all. It is really simply a wonderful time for our families to get together and celebrate. I also don't feel that I have to be in church to be close to God, which helps."

"I wouldn't refuse to go to church if she wanted to," Eddie commented. "In fact, I'm sort of curious about it and would find it interesting, I am sure. We have Christmas at our house, and all the in-laws come.

"To go into a marriage like ours, you have to be understanding toward others' views, and understanding toward your own background as well. I really think that it is a lot more demanding of you than if you married someone of your own religion, where you wouldn't even think much about it at all.

"When you express understanding for your partner in all of these religious decisions and matters, then there are no insurmountable problems in the marriage. In fact, I really think that being involved in an interfaith marriage has strengthened our relationship a lot. It has forced us to confront how we make decisions, and the importance of really demonstrating to your spouse that you care enough about her to listen to her views, try to understand her feelings, and figure out a way together that you can cope with all issues."

"I have created my own form of Christian belief," Heather

added. "The key to our relationship for me is the personal beliefs that we hold together. We use the word 'God,' which is universal for our own religious values, without having to say 'Jesus' per se. I think that helps a lot.

"I think that living together before we got married really helped us, too. I got to know him well and knew whom I was marrying by the time it actually happened. We also had an opportunity to see what each other's religious beliefs and practices were all about, so we'd know how comfortable or uncomfortable we were with them. That way, we had naturally discussed many aspects of interfaith life together prior to our actual marriage."

"At the beginning of our relationship our guards were up," said Eddie. "We were very defensive about our respective religions, and anything that the other might say or even ask about it. Almost anything could be taken as a possible hidden insult, or attack, or stereotyping of our religion by the other. With time, we built up enough trust in each other that we started to see the remarks and questions for what they were: simply interested remarks or questions designed to find out about each other and what we were all about.

"It really is a case of building trust between each other. I think *that* is the real key to the whole thing. I was concerned about a mixed marriage in the beginning, and only because we agreed to raise the child with experiences of both was I able to feel comfortable with the mixed marriage idea at all.

"Now we make decisions by never assuming anything. It's fifty-fifty. You have to agree to a happy medium, or the relationship will fall apart."

"It's important for each of us to express our views on things," added Heather, "and to listen and be tolerant of each other. You have to make decisions that are comfortable for both sides. Sometimes you just keep on fighting over something until someone is willing to compromise or give in. In the long run, we compromise on everything."

"Yes," Eddie said, "but you've got to be willing to really share how you feel with each other, even when you don't agree on something, or you know that it will create friction or tension between you. We share our differences and grievances with each other very easily. You *must* in an interfaith marriage, otherwise you will keep it inside and it will build up until it explodes in ways that you don't really like at all. Then it's worse than if you had only shared your feelings in the beginning."

"My rule is," said Heather, *"Nothing can be solved in silence."* Good advice, and a good model for *any* marriage.

Christmas/Hanukkah/Passover/Easter

Without a doubt, the primary area of discussion regarding religious rituals and celebrations revolves around Christmas. For some, the issue is whether or not to have a Christmas tree in a home that is predominantly Jewish in tone. This issue often arises within couples who have decided to raise their children as Jews, but where one spouse remains Christian and feels a strong yearning for the holiday symbols of *their* youth.

At times, this discussion continues long after someone who was not born Jewish has converted to Judaism as well. There is just something so very powerful about a Christmas tree that it captures the imagination of children for life. Those who have grown up looking forward to decorating it and joyfully opening their presents each year amidst its lovely fragrance and beautiful lights, often find it very difficult to eliminate from their lives.

It is usually the single most difficult religious symbol for most who were raised Christian to give up. For many, each December is a time of tension, conflict, and feelings of guilt and unhappiness, as they struggle to overcome their feelings of resentment and loss at no longer being able to recreate the most wonderful and positive memory of their entire childhood for *their* children.

For most of the individuals whom I interviewed, interestingly enough, the Christmas tree wasn't really a religious symbol at all. For most, it represented gifts, giving, warmth, love, family, the joy and excitement of the holiday season, and the expectation of wonderful family dinners filled with laughter and happy memories.

With this as the primary association to the tree itself, it is little wonder that the absence of the tree each year produces such sadness and despondency among so many who are involved in interfaith marriages. Parents want their children to have the same warm and loving memories that they had as children. For many, there is actually a feeling that they are depriving their children in some serious way of all the joy that *they* experienced as a child.

Often I have sat with interfaith couples as they shared the frustrations and arguments that they have suffered over whether or not to have a Christmas tree in their home. The Jewish partner is often strongly against it, saying that for him or her it is a clear symbol of Christianity, the birth of Jesus, and a form of betrayal of his or her Jewish roots.

For the born non-Jew, it is mostly a desire to recreate the wonderful memories of childhood, usually with little specific association with Jesus, Christian ideas of messianism, or even Christianity itself. In fact, it is precisely because of the lack of clear religious associations with the tree for the born non-Jew that they have a difficult time understanding the objections of their Jewish partners.

There is no magical solution to the Christmas tree dilemma. As with other decisions that a couple must make in their interfaith lives, deciding whether or not to have a Christmas tree in their home is a matter of expressing their true feelings, working together to discover the hidden longings behind those feelings, the source of guilt on both sides, and arriving at a decision together that both can live with.

There have been times when even I as a rabbi have suggested to a couple that they get a tree and see how they both feel about it. At times, the mere realization that it is usually impossible to recreate your childhood as an adult in such a totally different setting and life-style is enough to allow the non-Jewish partner to let the tree remain as a warm and *loving* memory.

Sometimes, the opposite happens, and both find that the tree is something that adds a dimension to their holidays that they desire and are comfortable with. For many, the tree becomes a symbol of the holiday season, and the explanations given to their children range from "It's a part of Mommy/Daddy's childhood that she/he misses and wants to share with you," to "We are making the tree a universal symbol of the holiday spirit, of light and tolerance and the love of our family," to "The tree is Daddy/Mommy's because he/she is Christian, even though the rest of us are not."

As a rabbi and a student of religion, it was one of the surprising outcomes of my research to discover how many people divorce the Christmas tree from Christmas itself, in the religious sense.

"My family always celebrated Christmas, just to give gifts, and Hanukkah as well," said Dan, who is Jewish. "We had a tree too because it was just a holiday symbol."

"The tree isn't really a religious thing anyway," his Catholic wife, Brenda, added. "It's the spirit of the thing that counts. We share both holidays. His mom buys us candy and eggs for Easter, too. She just likes any excuse to buy things. It isn't a religious holiday with my parents either. I guess it was more so when I was a child, but not anymore."

"We don't celebrate anything in a 'religious' way," said John, who was raised Lutheran. "The holidays are family times mostly, but we do tell our children about the religious aspects of them. Mostly I see them as just our joyous times together."

"The biggest issues with us were the raising of kids, celebration of Christmas, and whether or not to have a Christmas tree in the house," said Monica, who was raised Catholic. "We decided to have a tree for me. I think it lost its religious meaning a long time ago. For the material aspects of life we celebrate Christmas, and for the religious, Hanukkah, and we decorate for both.

"I get angry with people who tell me, 'You shouldn't have a tree in your home.' Even my mother-in-law says something about it each year like, 'I wish you wouldn't put it up.' Before I tried to discuss it rationally with her, but now I go for the emotional level. I will say to her, 'I enjoy it, it's important to me, and that's just the way it is. Other people will just have to live with my needs.' It's too bad that religious symbols push buttons so easily for people and they get so agitated about them."

"My brother-in-law doesn't want us to give him a Christmas present and tells us that we shouldn't have a Christmas tree," said Bobby, raised Presbyterian. "Well," added Rita, who was raised Jewish, "we celebrate Jewish holidays religiously, and Christmas as a gift-giving and family time."

"We celebrate Christmas in our home," said Deidre, raised as a Protestant, "and it seems to offend lots of Jews that we do. I said, 'We had a nice Christmas,' to someone in the office who is

Jewish, and he got upset because Aron [her husband] is Jewish. Yes, in my religion, it is the birth of Jesus Christ, but it's more so a time of giving, a happy time, and we have a very nice, happy Christmas. My memories as a kid are of filling our house with relatives.

"At Christmas we overload on presents. I love the lights, the tree, and the presents. We bring my mother and brother out from the East and go to my other brother's family and get lots of people together to celebrate. It's really my favorite time of the year."

Arthur, who is Protestant, told me that the biggest issue in his marriage to Pam, Jewish, is whether or not to have a Christmas tree at home. "We haven't had one yet, but we weren't married then. Now that we are married, I think I will want to have my own tree in the house this Christmas.

"As far as I am concerned, you really don't have to give up anything to be in an interfaith marriage. I associate Christmas with kids, family, getting gifts, and all being together. It's not really a religious holiday for me, and neither is Easter. Easter is simply a time for candy, Easter eggs, and for the kids and family to have a wonderful dinner together and celebrate."

Without question, for many interfaith couples Christmas and Easter become times primarily to "have a dinner and celebrate," without any specific religious overtones to the celebrations themselves. What appears to be celebrated is the idea of family, of sharing, of creating a moment in time each year to simply be together in a happy, joyous, festive environment, and perhaps be thankful for all the gifts and blessings that we have in our lives and relationships.

Carl, raised by a Catholic mother and a Protestant father, and Mindy, raised Jewish, are yet another example of this typical interfaith attitude toward the celebration of holidays.

"We don't have any religious symbols in the house, except a mezuzah on the door and a Hanukkah menorah," Carl told me. "We celebrate Jewish holidays with her parents, and Christmas at our house, although not religiously. It's really a family and gift-giving time.

"We try to give our daughter gifts every other night on Hanukkah, and then the rest under the Christmas tree."

What is interesting about this couple is that although they perceive their own celebration of Christmas as not "religious," and communicate it that way to their daughter, Carl admitted to me that he has a very different perception in his own heart.

"For me, in my heart it is religious, as is Easter. They are all in relation to Jesus and his birth, life, death, and resurrection." And yet, as part of the accommodation to the interfaith nature of his marriage, Carl has agreed all along to allow his daughter to choose her own religious identity (at the age of ten she told me that she was Jewish), and consequently kept the "religious" nature of Christmas to himself.

"I was uncomfortable with the tree and Christmas made me feel uneasy," said Michael, who is Jewish. "My mother used to say, 'Well, if you start with a tree, then it will be a cross, then pictures in the house of Jesus . . . ,' so I think about it each Christmas."

"I wouldn't have a cross in our home either," responded Michael's wife, Fran, who was raised as a Catholic but has since converted to Judaism. "We celebrate all the holidays and celebrate Hanukkah every night. The tree is just part of the fun of the holiday season. The truth is that Michael likes having it, because he never had one as a child in his home and it's fun for him. I can't just drop and forget everything from my past, so we made an agreement. We try to compromise—like I put up blue and white lights on the tree and make Jewish stars to hang on it."

This compromise is one that I discovered takes place in many interfaith homes. It is an attempt on the part of both partners to be flexible and figure out together how to have a tree for the born Christian while keeping the religious Christological overtones out of it. In fact the attempt, for the most part, seems to be to create a kind of Jewish version of the Christmas tree that will not offend the born Jew and at the same time allows the born Christian to keep a very important and special holiday symbol from his/her past intact.

With Andy (Congregationalist) and Michelle (Jewish), it was a case where the stronger will won. Andy felt that his religious upbringing provided a strong basis for a sense of family relationships within a community. Social relationships were the most important aspect of church affiliation, and he has always believed in God. Jesus, however, has been a confusing and much less clear aspect of his religious faith and commitment.

Michelle was raised in a very Jewishly involved family, with the celebration of Jewish holidays and rituals, and a strong connection with the Jewish community as an important part of her personal identity.

"I can't relate to church and Jesus and am uncomfortable with Jesus talk," she told me. "Church is such a foreign place for me that I can't share his experience."

"Well," Andy responded, "it's easier for me to go from one religion to another since God is the same regardless of Christ."

"We discussed Christmas before we got married [6 years ago], and I made my feelings very clear—I would not have a Christmas tree in my home. I felt that it is just inappropriate for me as a Jew to have one."

"It doesn't really bother me not to have a tree," Andy said. "It's pretty to have, but I don't need it. It's the same to me anyway, a kind of 'spirit of giving,' whether it's Hanukkah or Christmas. Besides, I've had it anyway, since we go to my parents' home each year, and *they* have a tree."

As we will see in greater depth in Chapter XIII, a partial solution to an interfaith situation where one partner feels very strongly about celebrating or not celebrating a holiday or ritual of the other, is to utilize parents or in-laws for a surrogate celebration.

Unfortunately, it's not always possible to simply ship your children or spouse off to the in-laws to take care of the holiday problem. Time and again I listened as couples shared the struggles and difficult decisions that they were forced to make, year in and year out, over which holidays to celebrate and how.

The tension over Christmas decorations, wreaths, and especially trees becomes a perennial problem for many interfaith couples. "The Christmas tree was the only religious issue we ever had," Adam said. "She wanted one so badly that finally one year she got one, but I wouldn't allow a real tree, just a plastic one and it didn't make her happy."

"Of course it didn't," Christy interjected. "It didn't satisfy me at all, and I was really miserable. It just didn't smell right."

Often couples try to figure out ways to both have a tree and not have one. In a sense, that is what Arthur and Pam are planning to do in their home. "Arthur really wants a tree," Pam told me. "The kids have received presents for Christmas and Hanukkah anyway, so we'll probably have a tree for Arthur. Lisa [a daughter] feels it would be hypocritical to have a family tree since *we* are Jewish, so it will simply be Arthur's.

"It really wouldn't bother me if we were alone. The kids are so steeped in who they are that it won't matter to them or confuse them in any way I'm sure, but it's still kind of an issue with us."

For some the issues are easily resolved, and for others the marriage becomes a lifetime of bargaining, negotiating, compromising, "giving up," being less than totally happy or satisfied.

"Holidays seem to be the biggest issue between us," Walter said. "I was born and raised Christian so all the Jewish holidays are new experiences for me. There is some overlap between them, but sometimes you have to make choices between one and the other.

"As I looked into the historical background of the various holidays, I discovered many of them are connected. That makes it easier for me to accept all the various holidays that we do celebrate."

Walter and Ruth celebrate Passover with a seder, for which they invite all the neighbors to their house and use the seder experience as an opportunity to discuss together the similarities between their Jewish and Christian backgrounds. They have created a celebration of the holiday that serves to bring them closer together each year, rather than pull them apart.

Whether it is Christmas, Hanukkah, Easter, Passover, or any other holiday or celebration that you share, the key element is in the *sharing*. The more you know about each other and your respective religious traditions, the easier it will be to fashion a shared religious life-style that adds significance and meaning to both your lives. Seek out opportunities to study, read together, attend lectures and seminars on each other's religion, go on weekend retreats with other interfaith couples, or join an interfaith-married support group through a local synagogue or church group.

Still, the most important issue for couples who must make decisions regarding whose holidays to celebrate and with whom, is the issue of open communication of feelings. In Chapter III, I discussed this issue at length, and as you can see, the ability to make decisions in a loving, supportive, nurturing, and sensitive environment is often more important than the actual decisions themselves.

I have spoken to interfaith couples who are happy and satisfied with their relationships who celebrate *all* religious holidays of both, who celebrate primarily the holidays of one or the other, and who pick and choose each year which holidays they will participate in as a family.

Obviously, the specific decisions that they make *do* have a significant impact on the health and vitality of their respective religious communities, be they Jewish or Christian. Those who are strongly committed to raising their children as Jews within the Jewish community, for example, have the most conflicts when it comes to the need of their partner for a Christmas tree, or other visible signs of Christmas in their home.

For many, there is a sense that the fundamental composition of the religious communities of America are in the midst of profound change. The breakdown of distinct barriers between communities, which has led to the increase in interfaith marriages in the first place, is also in part responsible for what may emerge as a new religious reality.

Whether specific traditional religious communities may like it or not, for a significant percentage of both the non-Jewish and Jewish world today, a new confluence of religious celebration and ritual that incorporates some symbols from both cultures is probably here to stay. For those religious institutions that respond openly and creatively to this new reality, interfaith families may become one of the largest and most interested populations for potential involvement and participation.

Creating your own religious life-style is one of the great challenges of an interfaith relationship. Don't feel that you are in it alone, for as you have seen, there are thousands of couples who are struggling with exactly the same issues that you are facing, and many of them are creating successful, loving, nourishing, and religiously satisfying lives together.

Keep your minds and hearts focused on the skills of open communication and the sharing of feelings and needs, and you will be successful too. Don't be afraid to seek out advice and support from outside sources, whether it is other interfaith couples, local churches and synagogues where there are programs especially designed to meet the needs of interfaith couples, or simply good friends.

The Importance of Friends

"It's nice to have friends to talk to and to go through it with," Jack said. "It's a way for us to find out about each other too, because of the questions that friends ask that we haven't even thought to talk about."

Interfaith relationships, as we have already seen, can be filled with generous amounts of both joyful experimentation and stressful decision making. Although each couple creates their own way to successfully deal with these stresses, there is one method of stress reduction that I universally recommend.

Going to therapy can be helpful to many, participating in interfaith support groups is beneficial, talking with a sensitive clergy person may be instructive, but without fail, one of the most important things that you can do for yourself and your relationship is *find yourself a friend*.

A friend can be invaluable as a sympathetic, *unemotionally involved* shoulder to cry on, or as an objective source for constructive feedback. A friend can tell you that you are overreacting to a comment or action of your partner, that your fears are simply the insecurity of entering into a relationship with someone whose background and cultural identity are different from yours.

A friend can be an invaluable help in keeping a perspective on your life and relationship that encourages you to build bridges of love and support, rather than construct barriers of fear and insecurity. Above all, friends help you remember that life is not lived in a vacuum. We live life with each other, with those we love, with those we work with, and with those we choose to share our lives with.

Each person with whom we come in contact has an influence upon us. This influence may be little or great, insignificant or profound, depending upon the quality and nature of the relationship itself, and the role the person plays in our life.

Choose to be with people who support you and the choices you have made. Choose to be with people who are open and honest with you, who are themselves good models of caring, supportive human beings, who can teach you to trust yourself and your decisions through their own experiences in life.

The more you *surround yourself* with positive people, the more positive you become. Likewise, the more you are around people who support the life-style that you have chosen, the more secure and confident you become that it is a life-style of value and worth.

Everything counts for something on the scale of your life, so the choices you make regarding how you spend your time and with whom are inevitably more significant than you at first imagine.

One of the problems we have is realizing the importance of the small things that we do in life—the little decisions, minor activities and associations of our everyday living. It just doesn't seem like a big deal that we choose to be with Sharon for lunch, even though she is always so negative about our life-style. She always seems to make us feel guilty about things we don't do that she thinks are so important, always compares her children to ours, her marriage to ours, her religious convictions to ours, in ways that almost seem designed to make us feel *uncomfortable* with our life choices.

After all, she *is* an old friend from high school, and we do have fun reminiscing about the good old days we spent together.

Every minute that you spend with Sharon is time tearing down your sense of self-esteem, your certainty that the life-style you lead is appropriate to your needs. Better to spend time with your other childhood friend, Jessica, the one who is always enthusiastic and positive, the one who is always excited about life and the different ways that people live it. Jessica is the one who, when you announced that you were going to marry someone of a different religious background, immediately said, "Wow, I bet that will be really interesting for you. Think of all the new and different things you will learn from him and his family. Sounds fascinating to me!"

It is the Jessicas in life who provide the reinforcement in our day-to-day search for validation. It is the Jessicas in life to whom we turn in times of doubt or despair for that little lift, that quick fix of positive energy. They're the ones who remind us of all the blessings we have in our lives and relationships, the gifts of love and family that really do fill our lives most of the time, and the manifold opportunities for discovery and joy that present themselves to us each day.

Yes, relationships like that are not always easy to find. When you have one, hold on to it for dear life. Protect it with all the resources at your command, for it can be a lifesaver in times of stress and need.

Such relationships are an important part of the support system with which you can face the trials and stresses that are a part of your marriage. If you don't have a Jessica in your life, find one. Sometimes if you are lucky, a relative, sibling, or parent can fill this function for you. Either way, one of the most important things you can do for yourself and your relationship is to create the kind of support system that will give you added strength, courage, determination, and resolve during those dark moments of doubt that will inevitably surface over the months and years ahead.

Part Four

CHILDREN
OF THE
INTERFAITH
MARRIAGE

Chapter XI

"BUT HOW WILL YOU RAISE THE CHILDREN?"

> "I was originally going to suggest exposing them to both, but I realized that it was really for my own ego primarily and not for the children's benefit. We both decided that our primary concern with regard to the children will always be what is in their best interest regardless of our own personal needs and feelings."
>
> —Monica, interfaith married four years

If there were no children, 90% of the arguments and disagreements in interfaith relationships would disappear. It's a strong statement, but based on the hundreds of conversations I have had over the years with interfaith couples, I suspect that 90% may even be an understatement.

Usually, adults are able to create an interfaith relationship based on mutual trust, respect, and tolerance. They usually have no trouble at all with the idea that they have their beliefs, and the person they love has his or her own.

I speak with couples all the time where one will tell me, "I'm Jewish and I celebrate Jewish holidays with my family, and my husband/wife/partner/friend is Christian, and we celebrate Christian holidays with his/her family."

185

Such couples abound and often have little tension and few problems in their relationship as a result of their different religious backgrounds. However, throw a child into the equation, and these same tolerant, flexible, supportive, and understanding adults often turn into hard-core religious chauvinists, who come roaring out of their respective religious closets as defenders of whichever faith they happen to be.

Most of the time, they surprise even *themselves* with the depth of emotion that they feel and express. Children bring out the sense of tradition in us all; they stir our ancient longings for immortality and remind us that we are part of a chain of humanity stretching back through aeons of time. Our own sense of personal history is piqued, and we find ourselves reminiscing about our own child-hood and planning all the exciting things from our past that we want to share with our own children.

In the midst of such bucolic reveries, however, individuals suddenly realize that their partner may just have very different ideas as to the childhood memories that he or she wants to share with the same child. That realization begins the process, which for many lasts through the entire childhood of their children, of negotiating the religious life-style that will be a part of their children's lives.

Making these child-related decisions is often the single most difficult task that interfaith couples must face. Unfortunately, there are no easy answers, either, for the world of interfaith marriage is a relatively recent phenomenon, and most couples must struggle to find their way alone. Most couples simply make compromises that will work at the time and hope that things will work out smoother as they have more experience with the deci-sions that they are forced to make each day, month, and year.

As we have already noted in previous chapters, one of the few constants in life that you can truly count on is change. Often I have seen couples make decisions and agreements with each other regarding the upbringing of their children, only to discover that when the reality of childbirth happens, and *their* living, breathing baby is resting in their arms, previous agreements melt like snow in the spring. We will see how some of these agreements have worked out in the reality of individual couples' lives later in this chapter, but first let's take a moment to consider some of the fundamental questions raised by couples who are faced with making interfaith child-raising decisions.

"How do we make child-related decisions?" I am often asked. Couples who were raised in different religions often are so timid with each other about the issues of raising children that, as with so many unexpressed feelings and emotions, they are loathe to discuss how they *really* feel for fear of estranging themselves from the person they love. You *must* force yourself to break through this barrier if you find yourself avoiding the conversations that in your heart you *know* are inevitable.

First you must decide if you are going to have children at all. In this day of dual-career families, of men and women marrying at later and later ages, the number of couples that choose *not* to have children is increasing. Still, the pull of biology, the inner, often not so quiet voice of nature calling to reproduce oneself, is a powerful enough force in most people's lives to lead them to decide to have children of their own.

The truth is that most people don't make conscious decisions about having children at all. They spend their entire lives growing up simply *assuming* that the natural order of the universe is that they become adults, get married, and have a family, usually in that general order. They never really question whether having children is something that they *want* to do, it is just something that they *expect* to do. And so, most of the time, most of them do.

Assuming that you are one of those individuals who have chosen to have a child, or perhaps without giving it a great deal of thought find yourself with a child on the way, you are obviously about to enter into a lifetime of important decision making. How will you make the decisions that you must make? How will you know what the "right" decisions are?

Most of the time, there is no one "right" decision in the first place. There are no magic formulas for raising the perfect child, there are only individual human attempts at doing the best one can for the safety, security, health, and welfare of one's children.

If there are parenting courses available where you live, whether from a local college or university extension, or a local church or synagogue, I strongly advise you to take them together. Somehow, "parenting" was just one of those many crucial courses left out of the standard high school curriculum, so most people have very little real information or helpful knowledge about how to be a good parent at all. They are simply thrown headfirst into the deep end the minute the child is born, and it's sink or swim.

Are Kids Confused by Two Religions?

Often it is more important how the discussions take place and how the decisions are made, than it is the specific content or the decisions themselves.

Regardless of the decisions that you actually make, however, there are some principles that are fundamental to any successful child-raising experience. What your child needs above all, more than any single other thing that you can give, is your unconditional love. Give your children a safe and secure loving environment in which to grow, where they will know that they are valuable, worthwhile, competent human beings who are capable of doing anything they choose, and of sharing themselves, their feelings, and their love with others, and you will be a successful parent.

Beyond these fundamentals, the reality is that when it comes to children in interfaith relationships, religious issues are decided in different ways by different couples.

Lori's parents came to a meeting of the minds easily. "I think it is important for kids to have a basic religious upbringing," Lee told me. "The philosophy of getting along with people and creating the kind of world we want to live in together is something that religion teaches, regardless of the particular religion involved. That, I believe, is the most important thing for kids to learn."

Judy added, "It could be confusing to kids if it's not clear up front. People have said to me, 'You're confusing your kids,' but the children understand our life-style and have their heads on straight. I know my kids, and we talk about it from time to time.

"It doesn't confuse them at all. They know who they are, who and what their parents are, what religions we celebrate, and feel that they are simply the product of parents who are from two different religious traditions. They get to have both of them in their lives if they want, and they see that as an advantage over others.

"When they were younger, they used to say often 'I'm half Jewish and half Catholic,' and I suppose that they would still say that if you asked them. The only decision that we made about religion was to leave it up to them. They sample whatever they choose."

The question persists among interfaith couples as to whether or not children are confused when growing up in a household that includes more than one religion. In general, the answer seems to be *no*.

When I began my investigation into the lives of interfaith married couples, I started with a belief that raising children with two different religious traditions could only be a confusing experience for everyone. Much to my surprise, I discovered that many children with whom I spoke (and you will meet some of them in the next chapter) felt absolutely no confusion whatsoever.

It appears that to a large degree the feelings that children experience, along with their sense of self-identity, are determined primarily by the attitudes and affective tone that is conveyed by their parents in their home.

Children seem to be confused when parents live lives of denial, confusion, secrecy, and avoidance of religious issues. When parents are open, honest, clear about their own beliefs, values, and patterns of celebration, children grow up with exactly the kind of security and sense of self-worth in the religious realm that I spoke of earlier.

For some parents, the lack of positive religious experiences in their own childhood is part of the reason they were attracted to an interfaith marriage in the first place. In such cases, it isn't surprising that parents often decide not to raise their children in any religion at all. Jack and Diane were just such a couple.

"We agreed not to raise them in a religious atmosphere because we aren't really religious ourselves," Diane told me. "I had one year of religious school [Jewish] and that was it. My mother said I needed to give them guidance, but I didn't have any, so I can't understand what she really means. We'll just see how it works with our kids as we go."

Jack added, "Our kids won't be confused because we don't compete religiously at all. We'll just explain to them whatever it is that we decide to do, if anything at all."

The other side of the coin is expressed by twenty-eight-year-old

Mary, who was the product of a Protestant mother and a Catholic father. The experience of growing up with constant religious tension in her home was so negative for her that when she married a Jewish man as an adult, she was willing to convert to Judaism to insure that her children would never go through what she had experienced.

"I was really confused as a child," she said. "If I chose to go to Catholic church my mother would feel hurt, and when I wanted to attend a Protestant church, my father got upset. I was always caught in the middle between them, and as a child wanting to please both parents, it was hell.

"Yes, I was definitely confused by the whole thing, but the confusion wasn't exactly over who I was, it was more a result of the lack of knowing exactly what was expected of me as a child. That was the most difficult part, 'cause I never really knew what I was supposed to believe, think, and do."

Mary's experience is typical of the caught-in-the-middle feeling that plagues many children of interfaith marriages. As a parent, it is your responsibility to give clear direction to your children, to let them know what is and is not expected of them when it comes to belief, religious values, rituals, celebrations, holidays, and the like.

"Leaving it up to them" will work *only* if the environment in which they are then raised is free of competing religions. It is not always an easy task to give your children the clarity of religious direction that is needed when you yourself are not sure exactly the direction *you* are going.

As Mary told me, "There is a conflict when you see one member of the family always going to church and the other never going. It sends you double messages, and as a child you don't know what is supposed to be important and what isn't. Our home was really not a religious home at all. Religion was avoided like the plague, and values were never discussed because they would open up a Pandora's box and lead to a religious discussion that was taboo. Thus I grew up confused over what I was supposed to be and do about religion, and turned off to it altogether."

Parental expectations play a major role in determining the overall attitudes of interfaith children. Do your children know how you and your partner/spouse feel about their participation in religious rituals, holidays, and celebrations? Do they think that either of you will feel hurt if they express an interest or desire to participate in or learn more about the religion of the other?

Such questions are fundamental to the attitude formation of interfaith children, and you owe it to yourself, your partner, and your children to discuss these issues as fully as possible so as to present a clear and united message to them, one way or the other.

Richard and Lisa, like many couples with whom I spoke, basically make decisions about their kids as the situations themselves arise. "We've never formally decided," Lisa told me. "We haven't given her (their 6-year-old daughter) any religious training yet."

"Not formally," Richard said. "We just answer questions as they come up. As of right now, we aren't involved formally with any religion. We had the only problems there have ever been in our relationship over making decisions about the children, so we didn't decide at all. I don't think we'll ever really have to decide. We just tell her, 'Different families do things differently.' "

This is one of the most common interfaith strategies—it's called "If I avoid the problem altogether, maybe it will just go away." It is, at best, of short-term value in any relationship. Avoidance is like a time bomb slowly ticking away. You never know when it will explode in your face.

The health and strength of your relationship demands that you confront the important issues and problems of interfaith life head-on. More important than the decisions you make together is that you *make* them *together*. Too many couples like Doug and Karen merely postpone the inevitable through a conscious strategy of avoidance. They may even conceal the fact that they are avoiding making clear decisions by identifying the pattern itself as a conscious strategy.

"It's a step-by-step process with our son," said Doug. "We take it as it comes. It's hard to sit down and make definite decisions, so instead we do it on an ongoing basis." Doug and Karen, like so many, are lulling themselves into a false security by thinking that "taking it as it comes" is a sufficient strategy with which to meet the serious issues of interfaith child raising. It will most likely prove to be confusing to their child if decisions are made in a haphazard manner, with no consistency to provide structure, security, and emotional boundaries.

A foolish consistency may be the hobgoblin of little minds, as the famous philosopher once said, but a wise religious consistency is often the salvation of childhood sanity. Treat your children with respect and give them a home with emotional stability and love. Don't create a family life that places your children in a no-win contest for religious loyalty between the religions of their mother and father.

Children have a right to stability in their lives, and parents have a responsibility to provide it. Children have a right to a sense of identity as well. They have a right to a sense of belonging to an extended family, a cultural heritage and a larger community that reaches beyond the boundaries of their immediate family setting.

Religion can be a force for strengthening the sense of self-worth of your child, creating a strong foundation of love and security, or, through conflict and indecision, can undermine those very values that are so necessary to a nourishing, supportive, and loving childhood.

Compromising Is Not Always Easy

Most of the conflicts that do arise among interfaith couples are a result of deep-felt needs for specific religious rituals and observances to be a part of an individual's life. Most people spend very little time dwelling on abstract religious principles. Their real concern is in the realm of "practical religion."

Baptism is a good example of where the conflict may arise between the practical and the theological. Arthur, for example, as a lifelong Catholic, found it unthinkable that a child of his would not be baptized. It just never entered his mind that anything other than baptism would occur. After all, the salvation of the innocent child's immortal soul was at stake.

Arthur believed that if his child *was* not baptized and something should happen and the child died, his or her soul would be trapped forever in limbo, unable to reach salvation with Jesus. That was simply an unacceptable alternative. He felt that since his Jewish partner didn't believe in the entire notion of salvation through Jesus in the first place, it shouldn't make any difference to her one way or the other. After all, Arthur reasoned, if I'm right the child's soul will be saved, and if she's right there is no harm done by simply having an extra ritual in the child's life. It seemed like a perfectly reasonable approach to him—a beautiful compromise.

Florence, on the other hand, saw baptism as a public symbol of making the child Catholic. At best she wanted her child to be Jewish, and at worst be able to choose for himself at the appropriate age the religion that he would follow.

Baptizing the child seemed so final, so definite, so clearly making a statement to the world (and to herself) that this child is now a Catholic baby. For Florence, this issue caused so much emotional stress and guilt that it was simply impossible for her to discuss it without becoming angry and upset. One person's "compromise" can be an unacceptable negative alternative to another.

Couples will often attempt to create a boy/girl compromise, or a "first one is yours, second one is mine" compromise. Too often, they have conversations within their own minds as they mull over the decisions that they would *like* to make regarding their children, and somehow forget to actually discuss the issues themselves with their partner.

Brenda was in the middle of sharing her views on child raising during an interview I was conducting with her and her husband, Dan, when she volunteered the following information: "If we have a girl I'd like her to be baptized, although I don't think I've told Dan that yet. Since I agreed to give a boy a Bar Mitzvah, I see it as a simple give and take."

Dan was surprised and a bit taken aback to hear this new piece of significant information that had just been dropped in his proverbial lap. He tried as best he could under the circumstances to find out what she really had in mind.

"I think our kids will be raised with everything," he said. "We'll explain the holidays to them and they'll decide for themselves. I really don't know enough about what baptism means to say anything about it at the moment. This is the first time I've heard about it and I'll have to find out what it means."

In what can only be described as a classic moment of understatement, Brenda replied, "Well, the priest just sprinkles some water on her and says a blessing and it's kind of a cleansing of sorts, that's all."

Obviously, Brenda and Dan have a lot to talk about, and it was sad for me to witness a not untypical demonstration of just how poorly couples really do communicate over these issues. It is simply sowing the seeds of disaster to avoid discussing these crucial needs, desires, and feelings with regard to the raising of your children.

Compromises grow out of a mutually supportive process. They are yet another example of how a team marriage is an important foundation for successfully negotiating your way through the potential emotional mine fields of the interfaith family. When couples aren't able to approach child-raising decisions as a team, they almost automatically become adversaries. Each decision creates a painful, unnecessary win/lose environment in which neither "side" feels totally good or happy.

David and Sylvia had been married for less than a year when they had their first child. David was Jewish, Sylvia was Catholic, and they had agreed in advance of the wedding (which was performed by a rabbi) that their children would be raised Jewish.

Unfortunately, their relationship was far from a supportive team marriage. In fact, David was so uptight and fearful that Sylvia would jump in ahead of him and "make the child a Catholic" that when he was checking her into the hospital in the middle of labor, he held up the entire check-in process until they changed the hospital form to read "Jewish" in the space marked "religion of mother," for fear that the baby would somehow look Catholic when it was born if its mother was listed as Catholic.

He then reminded Sylvia incessantly about her promise to raise the child as a Jew, and for the entire first week of the baby's life, made her promise every day that she wouldn't secretly have his new son baptized.

Sylvia, on the other hand, couldn't understand why he was so crazed about the whole thing. She thought David was the world's biggest hypocrite, since "He never goes to temple, he never celebrates holidays, and if I hadn't gone out and bought a menorah, we wouldn't even have been able to celebrate Hanukkah. I don't understand why all of a sudden he's so religious."

She was confused by his behavior, angry over the lack of trust he displayed, hurt by the constant harping on Judaism to the exclusion of Catholicism, and insulted that he then made arrangements for a Jewish baby-naming ceremony to take place in *their* home without even consulting her, or inviting anyone from her family.

Interfaith marriages need to be built on a foundation of mutual trust. Decisions about how to raise your children must be arrived at *together,* as part of a loving team where both partners feel good about the end results, or your marriage itself is being undermined from within. I suggest that if there is that much distrust and religious paranoia in the relationship, perhaps the marriage itself was not such a good idea in the first place.

How to Talk to Your Children

Conveying a positive attitude about religion and the religion of your partner is one of the most important gifts you can give an interfaith child. It isn't important what your respective religious beliefs are; what *is* important is the respect for each other and each other's beliefs that you convey to your child. The most effective parenting occurs when you teach by the example of who you are and how you act, rather than by what you say.

There are many different choices that you could make regarding the religious upbringing of your child. Regardless of the specific decisions that you may make, inculcating in your child a reverence for life, a sensitivity to the mystery and beauty of the universe around us, and an appreciation for the diversity of religious beliefs that add color and texture to the fabric of modern society *is* instilling a sense of religious values.

Should you let children decide their religious affiliation for themselves? Only if you truly don't care whether or not your children are raised with a sense of religious values and rituals. I am certain that you wouldn't let them decide for themselves whether or not to learn the alphabet, how to read, or the manners necessary to get along smoothly in society. You recognize that those are important fundamentals of living successfully in the world.

If you feel that an appreciation for the miracles of life that surround us, the ability to experience God and godliness in one's daily life, and *a belief in the reality of a world of being that transcends the ordinary* are important attributes for your children to possess, then you will treat the learning of religion with the same importance as addition, spelling, or writing.

By letting your child decide whether or not to have religion in her life, *you* are deciding no for her in advance most of the time. It is the rare child who actually chooses to attend a religious school, chooses to learn about religion and spirituality, or chooses to embrace rituals and religious practices in her life.

I have sometimes seen children choose to attend religious school against the desires of their parents, but it only happens when, through total luck or chance, their *peer group* of friends happens to be attending a given church or synagogue, and they simply want to be with their friends.

Most parents do not really want to leave the decisions regarding the total religious upbringing of their children in the hands of whatever friends the children happen to have at a given moment. In every other area of your children's lives, you communicate to them what it is important to know, to learn, and to do. If you let *them* make the choices when it comes to religion, you are telling them that it simply isn't important enough for the adults in their lives to make decisions about.

When kids *do* ask for religious training, I suggest that by all means you encourage them. Embracing religious values and customs can be one of the most enriching, satisfying, and emotionally important aspects of childhood when the child's family is open to and supportive of religious experiences. If children ask to go to church, let them. If they ask to go to temple, let them. Share with your children what is important to you, and your feelings about your own religion, while giving them the freedom to still make some of the religious choices in their lives.

Lori is a good example of how a positive and open attitude toward religion can truly allow a child the freedom of choice when it comes to religious observance or education.

Lori had been to a friend's Bat Mitzvah (the Jewish ceremony marking religious "adulthood" at age thirteen) and liked what she saw. "I thought I'd try and see what it was like for myself," she said. "My parents said that was fine, I could start Hebrew school, and if I liked it I could continue and have a Bat Mitzvah of my own.

"We don't really go to church, anyway. When I was younger I would go with my grandparents, but not anymore. Everyone is open to whatever I want, although my Catholic grandparents were sorry that I didn't follow the Catholic religion."

Lori did follow through with her Hebrew studies, her parents found friendships and satisfactions of their own through membership in the local synagogue, and Lori celebrated a meaningful and joyous Bat Mitzvah of her own. For most of her Catholic relatives, it was the first time they had ever been inside a synagogue, and her whole family used the Bat Mitzvah as an opportunity to get to know each other's religion and religious values better.

Even as Lori was celebrating her Bat Mitzvah, she told me that she didn't really feel that she knew enough about either of her parents' religions. Her Jewish background and training was stronger than her Catholic upbringing, but neither of them had been intensive or thorough, due to the interfaith nature of their family life, and the subsequent choices that her parents made regarding their own lack of religious ritual and celebration in their home.

This is a common situation for many interfaith families, and a common complaint that I heard from the children of interfaith marriages. "I don't really know much about either of my parents' religions" is typical of how such children often assess the level of their personal religious knowledge.

Often, at the same time that they will deny any feelings of confusion over their religious identity, they will admit that they really don't feel very competent in either religion, either. There seems to be a pattern of responses from the children of interfaith couples that indicates it is possible for children to be raised with both religious identities present in the house, and still not feel that there is much "religion" in their home.

When asked what religion they were, for example, Paul and Steven were unequivocal in their ambiguity. "I don't know," Paul responded. "I really don't have a religion. I guess you could say agnostic, since I don't believe in blind faith, but in just doing things the 'right way.' I need evidence to act or believe."

"When someone asks me that question," Steven added, "I ask them, 'Do you mean my parents or me? Do you mean origin, where my family is from?' I normally say I don't know what I believe. Mom is Jewish and my dad comes from a Christian family, but I am not really either."

Such a sense of being "neither" is a common result of being raised in an interfaith family. There are no guarantees in life when it comes to raising children. Interfaith couples must struggle with many decisions regarding the potential religious upbringing and values of their children, knowing all along that the results and effects will not really be evident for years, perhaps decades.

Creating a loving, open, honest home environment, where children feel free to make choices for themselves, try out different religious observances, and experiment with different religious identities in a nonjudgmental atmosphere is one successful model that many have adopted.

The religious choices that you make will, above all, set an emotional tone for your children as they grow. Think about the various real-life experiences that have been shared in this chapter. Read through the descriptions of individual family choices and life-styles, and stop after each one to see how you *feel* about them.

Read this chapter with your spouse or partner. After each example of a child-raising decision (or lack of a decision), discuss how each of you reacts to the choices that a given couple has made. Check out with each other any strong feelings that are aroused, memories that are stirred, or thoughts that are stimulated from experiences in your past.

Use these anecdotes as they are intended to be used—as vehicles to stimulate your own conversations, discussions, self-examinations, and decisions. Use other people's experiences as opportunities to examine the full range of your thoughts and feelings regarding the relationship between the raising of your children and your respective religious traditions.

The decisions that you make will determine a very important part of the formative experiences of your child's life. Take this chapter as an invitation to make these decisions in such a way that when you look back upon them in years to come, you will know that you have done your very best to insure your children a life filled with security, self-worth, and love.

Chapter XII

IN THEIR OWN WORDS—
WHAT CHILDREN SAY

"Yes, sometimes I feel like I am nothing, just celebrating every holiday on the calendar. But then I feel more Jewish on Jewish holidays and more Catholic on Catholic ones. There have been times I've felt like I have no religion at all, but it doesn't really bother me; I'm happy with what I am and in having the choice open to me to do what I want without pressure."

—Lori, fourteen, mother Jewish, father Catholic

Paul, the sixteen-year-old son of a Jewish mother and a Greek Orthodox father, described the dilemma of being raised in an interfaith family in the following way: "As a young child, you don't know what you are and don't have a chance to investigate your religion. People walk up and ask, 'Do you believe in God?' and you are forced to take a side, even when you don't know what to say. You end up giving them your life history, or you'll say, 'I don't believe in anything.' Then you hurt people's feelings so you say, 'Well, I'm kind of Jewish, kind of Christian.' Eventually, you just find a way of avoiding the question altogether as much as possible."

Paul is typical of a large group of children from interfaith marriages whom I interviewed. For some, like Paul and his younger brother Steven (whom we met in Chapter XI), being raised in an interfaith family has been primarily an experience of avoidance, denial, and the tension that arises from parents who did their best *not* to bring religion into their lives at all.

For others, like Lori, raised by a Catholic father and a Jewish mother who gave her the opportunity to participate in whatever religious training she desired, it has been a positive, exciting, and satisfying experience.

"I'm both," she declares without a hint of confusion or regret. "Lots of my friends are the same way, so it seems natural for me to be this way too. I think I have it good with both religions, and I feel more involved with both. I'm free to choose any religion, so I feel like I have a lot of freedom in my life. I see it as a positive thing for me growing up this way as a child. Now that I am fourteen, I can honestly look back at my childhood and say it was a very positive religious experience for me."

From these two examples alone, it is possible to see how widely divergent children's interfaith experiences can be. For some, it is an opportunity to learn about different cultures and religions, to participate in diverse cultural customs and rituals, and to feel fortunate to be a part of two cultural and religious worlds.

For others, it is a constant balancing act as they are poised between parents of different religions, and in-laws who each subtly push their own religious traditions every time a holiday or festival is celebrated.

The attitudes of children vary from family to family, even when two families seem to be raising their children with similar rules, attitudes, and agreements. Much has to do with the individual personality variables that are simply unavoidable, so that some strategies work well with some children, and the exact same strategies are dismal failures with others.

Unfortunately, there is no magic formula for successful interfaith child raising. Many children have grown up healthy, secure, with a positive self-image and sense of self-worth within interfaith families, but there doesn't seem to be one universal, simple, clear, step-by-step procedure for accomplishing this much-sought-after goal.

There are, however, some general rules that seem to apply across the board. Those children who seem to feel best about growing up in interfaith families have almost inevitably been raised by parents who are themselves comfortable with their own religious identities, whatever they may be.

It is the sense of personal security, of knowing who they are and what values are important to their parents, that seems to be the most positive result of clear communication from parents to children. When parents have made peace with each other over religious issues, when they have come to a workable agreement as to how they will live, celebrate, experience, and share religion and religious rituals and holidays in their home, *that* sense of security and stability is embodied in their children.

When Misty, age ten, wanted to comfort her Christian father one day, she turned to him out of the blue and said, "Don't worry Dad, you're like *we* are too." The "we" obviously referred to her mother (who was Jewish) and herself, and was both an acknowledgment that she saw herself and her mother as Jewish, and that she cared about her father's feelings, and wanted to make sure that he felt included in the positive attributes she associated with being Jewish.

Misty's statement was a reflection of her own positive self-image and signaled in a way her acceptance that being part of an interfaith family did not necessarily mean that anyone had to feel excluded or separated from one another.

When asked whether she will be Jewish or Catholic when she grows up, Cheryl, twelve, said without a hint of confusion, "It depends on who I marry. If he's Catholic and wants that, I will, and if he's Jewish that's fine too. I'm open to raising them like I was and letting them decide. I'm not big on heavy religion, going to services each week and stuff like that. The only thing we do is Passover dinner, Hanukkah candles, Easter, and Christmas. We go to grandparents' houses for those and celebrate the High Holidays, too."

Cheryl's is a good example of a typical attitude of a child raised in an interfaith family. Although she has basically positive feelings and associations with religion in general, and with the specific holidays that she celebrates with her family, she also has no *particular* religious loyalty or sense of identity. As far as she is concerned, she is perfectly willing (at least at age twelve) to put her religious future totally in the hands of whomever she eventually decides to marry.

Cheryl's attitude is widespread among children raised in interfaith families where the two religions and their respective holidays are both celebrated equally. In effect, if the intention of her parents was to raise her in such a way as to be totally open to either religion, and not feel any particular loyalty or specific identification with one or the other, they have been extremely successful. If, however, either parent was secretly hoping that she would feel more closely identified with their religion over that of their spouse, they will be sorely disappointed by Cheryl's response.

Children of interfaith marriages have many different feelings about their interfaith family life. For some it is seen as a bonus. As Alice, six, told me, "I like being different religions because there are more celebrations each year than people who have only one." Or as Erin, nine, who felt badly for those children who have only one religion in their home, told me, "This way I get to see what both religions are like."

For children, the positives that they feel inevitably revolve around the excitement of being able to celebrate more holidays, get more presents, and have more fun than if they only had one religion in the house. Tommy, eleven, is so proud of his interfaith status that he wears it like a badge at school. His idea of what an interfaith family was all about was, "I get to celebrate both holidays (Christmas and Hanukkah), and most of the other kids don't."

Some children identified religion as the major stress factor in their upbringing. Steven, fourteen, described his family life by stating simply, "Religion has been *the* key thing in our lives. When my parents got married it was a major factor and a big issue with them. They had a deal that the kids would be allowed to decide without pressure. But when one tries to "educate," the other thinks it's pressure, and they "retaliate" with their own ideas and religion.

"It's not only the parents either. It's their families, relatives, and all the rest. Everyone seems to have something to say about religion, or else they subtly push *their* religion when we are with them."

Being Caught in the Middle

One of the most common stress reactions that children express from interfaith marriages is the feeling of being "caught in the middle" between two parents, two religions, and two families. When I spoke to a group of children from interfaith families and allowed them to discuss openly their feelings, frustrations, and childhood experiences, they shared many poignant revelations.

Paul, sixteen, described the phenomenon of being caught in the middle in his life by saying, "It's been tough. It's not like it doesn't matter. When we are with each side, they are cautious to make sure that they aren't doing anything wrong. My parents say that they want their children to have free minds, but they really want their own way too, and that makes it tough."

Sharon, fifteen, said, "You can't be both. You're neither and stuck and don't really know what you are. You are afraid if you say you are one or the other religion that you will offend someone, so you figure out ways to avoid the subject and not get into situations where you'll have to answer questions at all."

"For me, it was more a sense of being ashamed that you didn't know than anything else," said Karin, fifteen. "Life after death seems to be one of the big religious differences, but as far as I am concerned, it is the person and not the beliefs that count in the world."

Many of these children echoed the feeling of "floating" from one religion to another (regardless of the specific religion of either of their parents) that Susan, fourteen, described. "I believe there is a God and all, and I practice different things all the time. I try out things and religions with my friends, first going with one, and then another. I'm always trying new things. I don't *need* to believe that 'This is the way,' and I don't think that there is one right or wrong religion."

The religious instability that comes with many interfaith up-bringings, the sense of wandering from one religion to another, trying on the religion of whichever friend happens to be around at the time, is one of the negative by-products that too often is a part of interfaith childhood.

Mary, twenty-eight, was the daughter of a Protestant mother and a Catholic father. She described first her parents' religious relationship, and then her personal reaction to it. "My parents were supposed to be married in a Protestant church. They had the minister all lined up, and then my dad's father refused to set foot in the church, saying, 'It's a sin.'

"They eloped and got married by a priest. My mother signed a paper saying that she would raise the kids as Catholics, but she never did. When her first son was born, she couldn't bring herself to go to Catholic church, so she took him to a Protestant church instead, and father wouldn't go. Then she did the same with me when I was born.

"My father went to Mass every week. My mother had no education about Catholicism and didn't like it for a lot of reasons. They had three kids, and then my mother had a hysterectomy as a result of a serious medical problem, and my father wouldn't have intercourse with her anymore in accordance with his strict understanding of his religion. After a year of fighting, and some violence, they finally got a divorce. I thought the whole thing was ridiculous.

"Three years ago my father got the marriage to my mother annulled so he could marry a Catholic woman in the church with a High Mass and everything. As you can imagine, my mother hates the Catholic religion and I used to hear lots of bad things about Catholics and conflicting things about Protestants as a child.

"Our home was always filled with tension, and when I got engaged to a Jewish man, I swore that I would never create that kind of conflict in my home for my kids. I took an Introduction to Judaism class and found that I really liked it. After the class I converted to Judaism and had a Jewish wedding."

Mary's experience is a perfect example of the destructive influences that interfaith marriage can have on a child when the home is filled with tension, stress, and religious conflict, and a beautiful testimony as to how important clear and consistent decisions *and* actions are when it comes to religion and your children.

Second-Guessing the Intentions of Others

One of the most insidious emotional games that is played by parents in interfaith marriages is called "second-guessing the intentions of others." This is a trap, born out of a relationship lacking in trust, missing the foundation of faith in each other and in the value of your agreements and decisions.

As one child told me, "My parents' tradition is really 'free thought.' They don't want any outside religious influences on me or my brother. Real pressure comes from a combination of our parents' perceptions of their in-laws, and the reactions and over-reactions that come as a result of those perceptions."

If you had trouble following that fourteen-year-old's line of reasoning, let me explain in plain English. The parents have made a decision that neither of their respective religions will be stressed, that the children will grow up free of "outside" religious influences, and that an equal amount of both religions will be formally celebrated in their home.

All is well and good, as long as there are no grandparents, cousins, uncles, or other extended family on the scene. Enter a set of grandparents, who at Christmas or Hanukkah give gifts to their beloved grandchildren, purely out of the goodness of their hearts and in the spirit of the season (whichever season they celebrate).

"Aha," says the parent whose in-laws have just graciously bestowed these gifts upon the unsuspecting children. "This must be a sneaky attempt on their part to introduce more of *their* religion into my children's lives. I certainly won't let them get away with that."

And so, the dutiful parent compensates (or in most cases *over-*compensates) by introducing an element of *their* own religion to counterbalance the perceived undue influence of the in-laws.

Now, if this all seems either silly or overblown, then you will probably never fall prey to this pernicious problem. But if you are perhaps nodding your head in agreement, wondering to yourself what devious thing the in-laws will try next, you too may be headed for religious and emotional child-raising overkill.

Time and again, young people told me of the overreactions of their parents to what appeared to them to be an innocent comment, invitation, or gift from one side of the family or the other. Interfaith parents tend to develop a case of religious paranoia, which if left unchecked and unconscious can lead to increased stress, tension, and pressure on your children.

Not everyone is out to steal the minds of your children, and it is dangerous and destructive to your sense of family security, togetherness, and well-being for you to think so. You must trust each other to uphold the respective sides of any agreement or decision that you make together.

If there is truly a problem with the in-laws (yours or your partner's), it must be handled *together,* as part of your team marriage. Call the team together for a strategy huddle and include your children in the team as well. Tell them and your partner your perception of the problem and devise together a strategy for dealing with it that will help bring you closer as a family and a relationship, not drive you apart with distrust, secrecy, or deception.

Advantages and Disadvantages

It is important to demonstrate to your children that religion is an area they can feel free to explore without the fear of emotional reprisals from one parent or the other.

"Freedom of religion" is a constitutional right that seems to be absent from too many interfaith homes. It is one of the great ironies of so many interfaith marriages that in the very homes in which religion is supposed to be an open, freely chosen, and nonpressured part of the children's upbringing, it often becomes exactly the opposite. Religious pressure is a subtle thing and as often as not comes about as a result of both sides overcompensating for their natural fear of stepping on the other side's toes.

"We don't really get pressure about religion from our parents," Steven said. "They try to say, 'It's your choice,' but they end up trying to second-guess the intentions of relatives all the time, and that adds its own pressure."

Even in this religiously stressed family situation, however, the children see that many positive benefits accrued to them as a result of being raised in an interfaith family. "It strengthened us overall," Paul said. "There are positive consequences that come out of it, since you are forced to think for yourself. We really feel that we have choice in our lives. I don't think there is anything wrong with being content either."

"Yes," added Steven. "Everyone wants stability, and I'm a little jealous of that. But Paul and I are very independent—others need 'God' to be stable and need to depend on outside things, but you have to be stable within yourself. That's really the most important thing, and that we learned from our upbringing."

Often the negatives that children of interfaith marriages expressed were related to a feeling of ignorance on their part of things that seemed "important," that it appeared "everyone else" knew all about.

Shelly, the daughter of a Jewish-Christian couple, told me, "Whenever I was invited to my friends' houses around any holiday time, I would be a little embarrassed that I didn't know what the holiday was really about. It just seemed that everyone else knew all about those things, and that I was somehow a little strange because I didn't. Sometimes I would even avoid going to a friend's house at all for fear they would realize how dumb I was when it came to religion."

"What Will You Do as an Adult?"

Frank, seventeen: "I'm going to put less pressure on religion, because we had a lot. I would let my kids choose what they want, 'cause that would be the right thing to do. There are always outside influences to help them choose anyway."

Sally, eighteen: "If I get involved in an interfaith marriage, I will sit down with my whole family early on—my parents, his parents, our brothers and sisters, everyone. We'll discuss these issues together, because that is what makes the most sense. I wish my family had done that because I think it would have cleared the air a lot."

Terri, fifteen: "I will never get involved in an interfaith marriage. I will make sure that I am the same religion as my husband because I don't want to put my children through what my sisters and I have experienced."

Danny, sixteen: "When I decide to get married, it won't make a bit of difference to me what religion my wife is. I can get along with everyone, and I think I have learned a lot of tolerance for others because of my own interfaith family. The only factor that would matter to me would be personality, although looks would help, too."

Peter, fourteen: "I would probably draw the line at baptism, because I don't believe in it, but otherwise, I don't think it would matter to me what religion my wife was. I'd make sure to decide all those things in advance though before I got married, 'cause it causes a lot of tension when you try to make up the rules as you go."

Lisa, fourteen: "I don't know what I will do. I will probably be open to different religious experiences since I enjoy going to both church and synagogue now. It depends on whom I marry. If he's Catholic and wants that, I will, and if he's Jewish, that's fine too. I'm open to raising children like I was and letting them decide for themselves."

These few examples of how children responded to the question "What will you do as an adult?" will give you some idea of the typical mind-set of children who are raised in interfaith families. Along with these responses came a few suggestions for parents as well. The children of interfaith marriages were eager to share their own advice with those who might become interfaith parents themselves some day.

Erica, sixteen: "Choose which religion you want and stick with it. It doesn't matter which one you choose, but choose one. It makes it a lot easier on the kid."

Guy, fourteen: "Let the kids decide for themselves. They can make their own decisions, especially if you give them the freedom to think for themselves. Just don't pressure them all the time."

Cathy, eight: "Don't fight about religion. It's confusing to hear your parents fighting about what religion you are, and it makes you scared, so don't do it."

David, fifteen: "If you haven't picked a religion for yourselves, let the kid decide and don't pressure him. Be free with religion so there are open options to choose from. We celebrate all the holidays in my family, and the child should get a bit of everything and decide for himself."

Shelly, sixteen: "Don't make your kid feel like she is nothing. Everybody wants to be something, to be called something, and it isn't good to be nothing."

Yes, it isn't good to be nothing. That sentiment was echoed by children of all ages from many different families. The ones who felt that they were "nothing" were those whose parents unsuccessfully tried to walk the tightrope of religious ambiguity. These were the families whose children told me, "You can't really be Jewish and Christian at the same time. My mother is Christian, my father is Jewish, but I don't know what I am . . . I guess I'm nothing."

What conclusions might be drawn from these comments, shared from the hearts of children who themselves are the products of interfaith relationships? Each of you will draw your own conclusions. Each of you will take those words that resonate with your own sensitivities and see them as validation of the positions that you may have already embraced.

Either way, remember that it is in the arena of child raising that your greatest responsibilities lie when entering into an interfaith relationship. Children are the innocent victims of your insecurities, indecisions, and desires to avoid conflict in your relationship, and it is your responsibility to be courageous enough to protect them from such victimization.

Give them clarity of thinking and decision making. Come to agreements with each other as to how they will be raised, the holidays and rituals you will celebrate, the identity you will give them, so that *your* children will not be the ones quoted in someone else's book as saying, "It isn't good to be nothing."

Teach them they are something, they are significant, they are important, and that the role of religion in your life and the life of your family is to add guidance, direction, ethical instruction, and a sense of spirituality *to the world*. In that way, they will experience religion as a positive force in their lives and grow up feeling secure, with a strong sense of their own self-worth and the ability to transcend the ordinary and experience the divine in their everyday lives.

Chapter XIII

GRANDPARENTS—OBSTACLES OR OPPORTUNITIES

"It's important to be strong and independent so that they know their advice is appreciated but might not be taken. We listened to everything that everyone said and chose for ourselves. You have to be your own person in the end."

—Bill, interfaith married four years

When I asked Jack and Diane about the holidays they celebrate, and the tensions or problems that arise in relation to these difficult annual religious decisions, they smiled exuberantly and responded, "We don't have any problems *or* tensions. In fact, it's easier for us than for same-faith couples."

Diane declared, "We go to his parents' house for Christmas, and my parents' house for Hanukkah. Of course, we celebrate them both at our house too. We light lights for Hanukkah together at home, put up a Christmas tree, and really share all the holidays."

"Yes, I agree," Jack added. "It's easier when you have different religions because you never have to choose between relatives—there's no competition."

Jack and Diane are not alone in their assessment of the virtues of interfaith holiday celebrations. Many of the couples with whom I spoke echoed their sentiments exactly. For these couples Jewish in-laws are available to facilitate the celebration of Jewish holidays and rituals, and Chrisuian in-laws are there for the Christian holidays.

This "surrogate" celebration pattern is one of the most common interfaith coping responses. Often the problems inherent in making choices between different competing religions, especially for the children, become more than any couple cares to deal with. The solution for many is simply to use the grandparents as convenient religious celebration facilitators. In this way they can eliminate the necessity to choose at all.

In most instances grandparents are more than delighted to be involved in the lives of their children and grandchildren in any way that they can. Particularly when it comes to teaching grandchildren their own religious heritage and customs, grandparents have a tendency of seeing this as their natural area of expertise.

It creates a smooth, tension-free way of resolving potential conflicts over what to celebrate, where, and with whom when couples can divide the religious celebrations so neatly and easily into "your side" and "my side."

Providing "surrogate religion," as I like to call it, has become one of the most important roles that grandparents can play in an interfaith family structure. No one lives in a vacuum. Every interfaith family is made up of an extended family structure that includes brothers, sisters, cousins, parents, and grandparents representing different religions and cultures.

The most effective, tension-free use of this extended family is often found to be in this important area of surrogate religion. When grandparents are willing to serve as religious role models for their grandchildren, without placing undue religious demands on the parents themselves, it is often greeted with a great sense of relief and gratitude.

Time after time as I interviewed interfaith couples, it became clear that while they had made an overt agreement not to bring a particular religion or ritual into *their* home, one or the other partner was delighted that their children had the benefit of grandparents who would celebrate, teach, tell stories, sing songs, and demonstrate particular holiday celebrations and rituals in *their* home.

As grandparents become surrogate religious role models, they take on the task of passing down religious values, symbols, rituals, and history that the parents feel constrained from doing themselves. At times this occurs openly, with the clear assent and blessing of the parents. At other times, it comes across almost as a subterfuge on the part of one parent, an attempt to subtly expose the children to more of their particular religion than they had agreed upon in the first place.

When this happens, you are asking for trouble. Anytime there is secrecy, manipulation, subterfuge, or deceit in a relationship, you are undermining the foundation of your lives together. In addition, you are teaching your children by your example that the proper way to behave within a loving relationship is to lie or subtly deceive your partner. I don't suggest this as a positive act of role modeling for your children.

As with every other aspect of your marriage, it is the openness, honesty, and integrity of the communication between you and your partner that is of utmost importance. Be open with your needs and desires. If you want your children to celebrate Christmas, but have agreed not to have a tree in your own home, discuss it with your spouse or partner. Tell them what *you* want and suggest that if they still are uncomfortable having a tree in their (your) home, you suggest going to your parents' with the kids each Christmas so that they can experience the joy, beauty, family warmth, and togetherness that you experienced as a child.

In that way, you won't feel as if you are cheating your children out of one of your most cherished childhood experiences, and at the same time you maintain the integrity of your marriage by assertively stating what you want and how you suggest getting it.

This is a healthy interfaith response to a potential problem. Be open with yourself, your spouse, your parents and in-laws. There is nothing wrong with using them for surrogate religion, as long as you let them know that's what you are doing. Give them the respect, freedom, and opportunity to be a part of your religious family planning experience. Who knows, they may even have some good ideas and suggestions that will make you both feel better about what you are doing.

Invite your parents and the parents of your partner to your

home one evening. Sit down with them, and as Terri and Jim did, say to them, "We need your help in making the fact that we are an interfaith family work as a positive in your grandchildren's lives. We have been thinking very hard about how we can best give our children the greatest sense of family security, love, and values in a unified form, while at the same time giving them the benefit of the two diverse religious and cultural heritages that are their inheritance.

"We have decided that the best way to do both things at the same time, while remaining consistent in the celebrations and rituals that we have agreed to have in our own home, is to ask all of *you* to help us by being sources of surrogate religious training for them."

Surrogate religious training is one of the most constructive uses that interfaith couples make of their parents. I have noticed from my own discussions, interviews, and observations that the vast majority of the time grandparents are *delighted* to be used in this way. It helps give them a sense of purpose and makes them partners in the raising of your children. Providing surrogate religion can be a source of great joy, satisfaction, and meaning for the grandparents, and they are usually extremely pleased to be asked.

Keeping Your Marriage in Perspective

No matter how old we become, no matter how successful, competent, "important" in the world of business, finance, education, or society, there are moments in our lives, when we feel that to our parents we will always be nothing more or less than their children.

As an adult involved in an interfaith relationship, you have most likely made decisions that were not always in conformity with the wishes, desires, and life-style of your parents. Inevitably this creates tension and anxiety between you and, for many, may very well produce feelings of guilt as well.

Learning to relate to your parents as an adult, learning to develop a mature, adult relationship with them, free from the emotional encumbrances of childhood, is one of the important tasks of growing up. It is up to you to create a relationship with your parents based on mutual respect, intellectual integrity, and religious honesty.

Parents want to support their children. They want to be a part of your life and, if you have children, to be a part of their lives as well. It is often confusing for parents of interfaith couples to observe the life-style of their children and grandchildren, since they rarely have open, adult discussions about religion, ritual, religious philosophy, and theology with them.

If you take the time to share with your parents the rationale behind your own life-style choices, the reasons why you do and do not celebrate holidays, rituals, life-cycle events, and religious observances, it will go a long way toward giving them an understanding of the choices you have made. If you want them to be supportive of you and your religious decisions, be open with them regarding the priorities in your life and your attitude regarding religion, your relationship, and your religious life-style.

It's important for you to be conscious of the ways in which you slip into the child role with your parents. Especially in an interfaith relationship, you must be careful to protect the integrity of your adult relationship with your partner and not allow your childhood programming to undermine the adult choices and decisions that you have made together.

Your relationship with your mate is the most important and primary thing in your life. All else flows from it. You and your partner, and the team that you create, must always take precedence over the feelings, dreams, frustrations, upsets, tantrums, or scoldings of your parents. It is up to you to protect your partner and your children from your parents if necessary. Do whatever you can to create a loving, supportive, and cooperative relationship with your parents and in-laws, but at all times keep your relationship in perspective and your priorities straight.

Including parents and in-laws as important parts of your lives and the lives of your children is an effective way of creating a positive and supportive relationship with them. Do what you can to make them feel important, listened to, used as resources for surrogate religious training, as teachers, and as role models. Give them an opportunity to be an important part of your life, but always be clear that you are an adult with the right to make your own decisions according to *your* perception of what is best for you and your family, and you will not be open to emotional blackmail.

"We just don't talk about religion with them," said Judy about her parents and in-laws. "We humor both sets of parents. If a question arises from my family about our life-style or the religious choices that we have made, I simply try to answer it as best I can without bringing Lee into it at all."

"Actually, Judy's parents have never discussed religion with us together at all," Lee added. "We don't feel it is appropriate for them to get involved with our decision making. We don't discuss it. We just tell them in as matter-of-fact a way as possible what is happening and any decisions that we might make that affect them, and that's the end of the conversation."

"Even if Lee were Jewish, it would be the same," Judy maintained. "My best advice to people in interfaith marriages is, 'Live your own life,' period! Yes, of course, you want good relationships with your parents and your in-laws, but in the end it is *your* life, *your* relationship, and *your* children, and you have to live with your decisions, *not them*."

Judy and Lee's are typical of the attitudes that prevail among interfaith couples—keep a proper perspective on your relationship vis-à-vis parents and in-laws and remember that your life is up to you, not them.

Sometimes the preconceived ideas and perceptions that you have of your parents and in-laws has a significant impact on your relationship with them itself. Often interfaith couples shared their perceptions of the differences in their backgrounds and upbringing, as well as their expectations for the kind of relationship they could expect with their parents and in-laws, in terms of the differences they saw between their respective parents.

Dan described the differences between their families by referring to their mothers. "Our mothers are so different—it seems like my mother gives more. *Jewish families want to be more involved with us.* I just expect my in-laws to buy me something for our new house and they haven't."

Brenda actually shared his appraisal of the situation and felt that there *was* a greater sense of personal and family involvement with her Jewish in-laws than there was with her own parents. "His parents immediately gave us blinds, a fan ceiling lamp, and are real involved with us. I have a friend who's Catholic and wealthy and her parents, too, didn't offer to pay or help with things. Jewish families are more involved in general, and more giving. I don't know why, that's just the way they are."

Now it doesn't really matter if their individual perceptions are true or not. As long as they both *feel* this as a significant difference, it colors their views of their respective families. Often there appear to be subtle ethnic stereotypes that the couple have adopted and in a sense imposed upon the picture of their parents. These images can exert a powerful influence upon how each partner in the marriage will perceive the other's parents.

It is a truism among psychologists that "as you think, so shall you become." In a sense, *this self-fulfilling prophecy* is equally powerful when it comes in our relationships with others and our expectations of them and their behavior in a given circumstance. Brenda and Dan have created an expectation that her Catholic parents are "cheap," while his Jewish parents are "generous and forthcoming." This preconception may in fact prevent them from recognizing acts of largess on the part of Brenda's parents when they do occur.

In every relationship, whether casual or serious, we form impressions and make judgments of others. Often our initial perceptions of them stay with us long after our *experience* of them demonstrates a different or even opposite quality or personality characteristic. The same is true for in-laws, and in a marriage these initial judgments and perceptions can actually get in the way of breaking down barriers within interfaith families.

It is important to be aware of this phenomenon and guard against making lifetime decisions about your in-laws on the basis of initial impressions or actions. Remember, in every relationship there is a period of adjustment, of becoming comfortable with different life-styles, values, backgrounds, and social practices, and this process may take much longer than you think. Keeping your marriage in its proper perspective with that of your parents and in-laws may also require that you suspend initial judgments of others, and be open to new ideas, suggestions, and religious experiences.

So too with parents and children. When a new person enters a family system, there is an inevitable period of adjustment and acculturation into the new family. Typically, whichever family is more involved on a daily basis with the life of the couple exerts a greater influence over them and adjusts quicker to their own habits. This means it takes an extra measure of patience and understanding with the parents who are not as frequently a part of your daily life. As with nearly every aspect of an interfaith couple's marriage, the key concept is flexibility, tolerance, understanding, and of course communication to create the kind of relationship that you want.

Avoiding Parental Sabotage

There are times when the best intentions of you and your partner blow up in your face, and a religious event or observance will touch off a torrent of hidden emotion in your parents or in-laws that neither you nor they even knew was there.

It is not uncommon for parents of interfaith couples to bury their true feelings deep inside in an attempt at avoiding a fight or unpleasant scene with their child at the time of their decision to marry. Often there are feelings of hurt, rejection, and religious betrayal that have been denied for years, even to themselves.

Such deep-seated emotions may burst onto the scene years after the initial marriage itself, as if an emotional button was released by a significant moment in your life or the life of your family. These are moments when what may appear to be a simple thing becomes blown all out of proportion, until the entire family is in profound crisis.

Such was the case when an entire family crisis erupted over the simple naming of a child. The child's name became a symbol of rejection, loss, mistrust, prejudice, and estrangement.

Sheila had given birth to a beautiful baby boy just one week before, and it *should* have been an occasion of great joy for everyone. The trouble began, however, the very day of the birth, when Sheila's mother called her daughter in the hospital to find out all the wonderful details of this joyous new blessing in their lives.

In the midst of the conversation, Sheila's mother naturally

asked what name they had chosen for their new son. "We have named him Kristopher," Sheila replied, and her mother dropped the phone.

"Christopher!" she screamed at her daughter. "How could you name my grandson Christopher? You're calling your son *Christ*. Didn't you think that name might hurt me? Of all the thousands of names in the world, you had to pick the most Christian name in the entire book?"

"Well," the stunned Sheila replied, "we're spelling it with a *K*, and I didn't really think about it."

One thing led to another, and when her father picked up the phone and began *his* complaining to Karl, Sheila's non-Jewish husband, he hung up on her father and never wanted to see him or her mother again.

Karl thought it the ultimate arrogance for his in-laws to think that *they* needed to be consulted before *he* chose a name for his son. Sheila had told him that he could pick the child's name. She didn't really think it was that big a deal and was hurt by her mother's response. Meanwhile, the grandparents were devastated by the whole affair.

Ultimately, as I spent time with them in my study, we discovered that the depth of Sheila's mother's reaction to the name was a result of the fact that she had been denying all along that her daughter had truly married someone of a different religion.

The entire time (this was her daughter's second child), she had rationalized one thing after another (since the doctor who had performed the circumcision on the baby was Jewish, it was close enough to a "Jewish ceremony" for her, etc.), but now with the name Kristopher staring her in the face, she could no longer keep denying the truth.

She was experiencing a real sense of loss, of grief akin to that of a death, a sense of having lost something that in truth had existed only in the fantasies of her own mind—namely, a Jewishly involved and identified daughter.

Sheila couldn't understand the depth of her mother's feelings at all since they seemed way out of line with the severity of the "offense." After all, to Sheila, the name was "just a name."

The non-Jewish husband had felt an implied pressure all along to bring some Jewishness into their home. Since his wife's parents were the only grandparents around, they had a significant influence on the celebrations and "Jewishness" of his family anyway.

In his own mind, he heard the upset over the naming as a rejection of *him,* and even told Sheila that he heard her father say that he would never accept him because he wasn't Jewish. This further estranged her from her parents and put her in the untenable position of having to choose between her parents and her husband.

Working with Sheila's parents helped them come to grips with their sense of loss and grief and confront the reality of the limits of their influence over the lives of their children and grandchildren. Only when all of that had been worked through were the grandparents willing and ready to reconcile with their daughter and son-in-law.

The grandparents came to realize that they were ultimately responsible only for their own actions. They decided to first design in their own minds the kind of relationship they wanted to have with their daughters, their grandchildren, and the non-Jewish spouses of their children (since both daughters had married non-Jews), and then *act* in such a way as to create that kind of relationship.

It is so easy for emotions to get out of hand when you fail to communicate successfully or adequately with parents and in-laws about religious rituals and issues. Time after time the birth of a child, and the resulting religious rituals that accompany that birth, turn into moments of anger, frustration, and upset.

"When our daughter was born, my grandfather planned the whole naming," Rita told me. "He wanted Bobby to do something in Hebrew, even though he isn't Jewish, but he just told him what to do and didn't really take the time after that to sit down with us and talk the whole thing through.

"I was so uptight about the whole thing that I couldn't really deal with it effectively, so I just did nothing. What happened was a disaster. Since my grandfather planned it all, Bobby got angry and felt left out."

"I got angry not because he planned it, but because of how I was treated during the whole thing," Bobby explained. "It was important to him to have his great grandchild named with a Hebrew name in a Jewish ceremony, so out of respect for him I spent lots of time learning how to say a prayer phonetically in Hebrew. Then, when the ceremony actually happened, he complained that he didn't like the way I said it.

"I blew up at that and said, 'That's it. I'm never doing anything like this again.' I felt very badly treated, like I was a second-class citizen at my own child's ceremony, and I resented it."

Learn a lesson from these examples. Take charge of your relationship with parents and in-laws. Use the grandparents constructively, involve them in your life and that of your children, but do so on your own terms, with clear and understood guidelines and expectations.

Learning to cope successfully with the needs and emotions of parents and in-laws is one of the necessary life skills that interfaith couples must cultivate. Creating the team marriage, *which allows you and your partner to see the world and the myriad decisions that you both must make through the lenses of your relationship first,* will go a long way toward creating a sense of emotional security and strength in your marriage.

We change over time. As parents, as children, as partners in relationships, we all must be open to our growth and that of the significant others in our lives. In this way, as the words of the Bible tell us, "The hearts of the parents will turn to their children, and the hearts of the children to their parents."

WHEN THINGS DON'T
WORK OUT

Chapter XIV

BREAKING UP AN INTERFAITH RELATIONSHIP

"What is said easily when things are going great and they are feeling in love with each other doesn't always set so easily when there are struggles or tension or even a divorce going on."

—Bill, interfaith married four years
for the second time

The entire thrust of this book has been to share as many ideas, strategies, and firsthand experiences of interfaith life as possible, and to help those who have chosen an interfaith relationship to prosper, grow, and succeed in their lives together. The sad reality, however, is that in spite of the best intentions and plans of every couple, many end by breaking up their relationship.

Just as marriages can be either successes or failures, so too can divorces. A divorce is a success when both parties end up with dignity, sense of self-worth, and ability to cope successfully with the challenges of life intact, or even enhanced.

With the statistics for divorce in America reaching astronomical proportions, it comes as no surprise that interfaith relationships suffer at least as much as same-faith relationships do. In fact, there is some evidence to suggest that interfaith relationships fail at from three to six times the rate of same-faith marriages.

My purpose in this book is not to debate the pros and cons of interfaith marriage. Neither is it my intention to quote the studies and statistics that suggest that choosing an interfaith relationship increases dramatically the potential stumbling blocks and difficulties that you will face in creating a loving, supportive, mutually satisfying marriage.

On the other hand, it would be foolish to ignore the reality of interfaith divorce, and the specific issues and problems that tend to be a common part of the interfaith divorce experience. This chapter, therefore, will briefly suggest a number of specific concerns that I believe must be confronted to successfully weather the storms of breaking up a marriage, while at the same time protecting both your own integrity *and* the religious integrity of your children.

Way back in Chapter IX, I pointed out that one of the common experiences of interfaith marriages is that ordinary tensions and stresses in the relationship tend to be mistakenly seen through the ever-present prism of the "interfaith" nature of the relationship itself. *Every* problem is not the direct result of differences in your religions. In fact, most of the time, it seems to have been the couples I spoke with themselves who superimposed the interfaith umbrella over issues that in same-faith marriages would have no "religious" overtones whatsoever.

In relationships in which differences in religion seemed to be a major cause of the breakup, there was a marked inability on the part of both partners to dissociate their religious identities from the daily tensions and upsets of their lives. It was in such relationships that I heard over and over, "I just didn't realize how different our religious backgrounds made us."

For some it was a slow buildup of resentment and irritation, brought on by casual remarks, family impositions, or disagreements over how to raise the children. "I was bothered every time Jill would say something like 'Jews always seem to know how to handle money,' or ask 'Why do Jewish parents always have to be so nosy about their kids' lives?' " Marvin told me. "I just couldn't bring myself to say anything to her about it because it seemed so petty on my part, but it really bugged me."

Jill, on the other hand, thought that Marvin was unpredictable and moody and never knew when his mood would suddenly turn sour. "He used to get quiet all of a sudden and go into another room without telling me why," Jill said. "Even when I would ask him what was the matter, he'd just shrug his shoulders and tell me that nothing was the matter and then read the paper or watch television. It was frustrating never knowing what set him off, or when he would decide to become upset about something. Half the time I was married to Marvin, I felt like I was walking on egg-shells."

Although their lack of adequate communication skills is glaringly obvious, it is worth noting that what kept upsetting Marvin were remarks that he interpreted as being anti-Semitic. The buildup of resentment toward Jill that he felt over the years simply added fuel to whatever fires of discontent were already burning in his psyche.

Whatever the ultimate "reason" for the breakup, and I suspect there is never *a* reason for the disintegration of a relationship, but rather a series of confluent processes and experiences that lead to separation or divorce, there are still ways to maintain the self-respect and dignity of everyone involved.

First, avoid attacks on your mate's religion at all costs. It is just too easy to say, "I should have known that a _____ (fill in the blank with your ex-partner's religious persuasion) would act like (or say or do) this." It will only serve to aggravate the situation and deflect from whatever real issues may need to be dealt with between the two of you.

This is particularly crucial if there are children involved. It is the universal tendency of couples who go through a divorce to bad-mouth their ex-spouse. It often takes a great deal of self-discipline for such ex-spouses to force themselves to refrain from casting aspersions upon the good character of the person who is still their children's father or mother.

Under any circumstances such negative comments only come back to haunt the one who gave them voice in the first place. The old saw "Every knock is a boost" was never so true as in this particular instance. Your children will still love and need their other parent whether you do or not. Putting down your ex-spouse will only make *you* look petty and vindictive in your children's eyes, and paint your ex as the victim of your uncontrolled wrath.

If this principle operates in divorce between same-faith couples, it is even more true in the case of interfaith relationships. Children in interfaith divorces are subject to a potentially confusing assortment of religious decisions and choices. They often feel (or are made to feel) that they must choose sides, not only between Mommy and Daddy, but between one religion and the other. It is particularly cruel to force such decisions and feelings upon innocent children, and it has the potential of turning them against *any* religion whatsoever in the future.

Even small children know what is going on and understand much more of what you say and mean than most people give them credit for. "It was awful," Kris, aged six, said about his parents' divorce. "They used to yell a lot, and Daddy would say bad things about Christians to Mommy. I was scared that he would yell at me too if I said I wanted to see my friends at church."

Kris, who up to age six had been "raised as both Jewish and Christian" by his parents, began to feel great anxiety anytime Christianity or church was mentioned during the time of his parents' divorce. He was afraid he would lose his father's love if he showed any interest in the friends he had met at church, and was torn by his need for the protection and love of both his parents, who seemed to demand his loyalty to different religions at the same time.

Avoiding attacks on religion is important both as individuals and as a couple, for it allows you to focus on whatever the true sources of stress and dysfunction are in the relationship, rather than being deflected into the emotionally safer ground of religious stereotyping. This strategy works best if you can sit down with your partner and mutually agree to stay away from discussions of religion that merely affix blame or direct accusations toward each other. The breaking up of a relationship is painful enough without confusing the issues or stirring up your emotions even more by throwing religion into each other's faces.

In most relationships religion alone is rarely the cause of a breakup or divorce. I have found that religious issues are usually only symbolic representations of the underlying problems and differences that drive relationships apart, and become a useful scapegoat for the frustration, anger, disappointment, and sense of failure that inevitably accompany the dissolution of a relationship.

In a divorce or breakup of a relationship, with emotions under high pressure and stress, it is especially important for you both to be able to think as clearly and dispassionately as possible.

When that is simply impossible for one or both of you, you might consider finding an objective third party to act as the go-between. Today, there are many places that you can go to find such a person or persons, once you decide that you are willing to seek such help.

First, you can seek the aid of a therapist or counselor. Many are available at very nominal expense or work on a sliding scale according to your ability to pay. A good place to look is the local United Way agency directory. There are many counseling centers in practically every city, whether sponsored by the local family service agency, churches and synagogues, or various ecumenical and interdenominational associations.

Second, there is a growing field of service to individuals and couples called divorce mediation. Within this general rubric are often services that combine lawyers, counselors, clergy persons, finance consultants, and any other professional service necessary to facilitate the smooth resolution of the inevitably difficult decisions that every separating couple must make.

If you have both developed a relationship of trust with a particular priest, minister, or rabbi, this may be an excellent time to make use of their services as well. These are the kind of people who are there to help you through what is often a very stressful experience. Use whatever resources are at your disposal, and if you don't know of such resources, *find them*. I guarantee that they are there, available, and eager to help if you but ask.

Custody Decisions

Inevitably when it comes to divorce or separation, the most sensitive and difficult issues to resolve are those dealing with children. It is natural to channel our frustrations and anger over an unsuccessful relationship through the decisions that are reached over the continued living arrangement and raising of the children.

This, too, is a dangerous trap. Kids are to be loved, cared for, and protected, *not* used as a weapon to "get back" at an ex-partner for all the nasty, rotten things that he or she did to you in the past. Too often I have seen couples use their children as emotional footballs, forever tossing them back and forth, as if *their* feelings must take a backseat to the opportunity to vent one parent's anger at the other.

The simplest, most easily understandable rule to follow when making decisions that affect your children is: Do whatever is in *their* best interests, whether it is in *yours* or not. Simply ask yourself the question "What is the best for them?" and the answer will be your guide.

There may be times when doing what is best for your child will seem to be the most difficult and painful decision you have ever made. It is precisely at such moments that you must remind yourself of the responsibility that you assumed the day your child was born.

Being responsible for the emotional nourishment, intellectual development, and spiritual growth of your child doesn't end with the marriage. It truly is a lifelong task simply made all the more challenging and complicated by the breakup of your relationship.

There may indeed be times when the best decision for your child is for him or her to be with your ex-partner more than with you. The willingness and ability to make that decision is not an abdication of your responsibility, it is rather a mature *expression* of that sense of responsibility.

Every divorce, like every marriage, is an opportunity for growth and discovery. The challenges of creatively deciding upon issues relating to the custody and upbringing of your children provide perhaps the best opportunity for stretching your ability to make mature, sensitive, appropriate choices while in the midst of one of life's most stressful experiences. See it as the opportunity and challenge that it is, and it will help you to make the right decisions.

One of the most helpful strategies for dealing with child-related religious decisions in a divorce is to make formal, written agreements regarding the religious education and upbringing of your children. Writing down on paper your expectations regarding the religious training and holiday and ritual celebrations that your child will participate in will greatly reduce the possibility of arguments or misunderstandings in the future.

The benefit of such formal, written agreements is so widely recognized that in many states they form the basis of legal decisions related to specific custody arrangements made by the courts. Because this is increasingly becoming a normal part of the legal proceedings within divorce agreements, many couples are attempting to eliminate even the possibility of a disagreement or misunderstanding ever arising by writing a prenuptial agreement concerning the religious life of any potential children.

Prenuptial agreements do have certain advantages. First, they are made at a time when the couple are in love, supportive of each other, and can easily reach a mutually shared understanding. It is always better to make important decisions when not under the added stress and mixture of emotions that accompany the turmoil of a relationship breakup.

Second, it forces the couple to talk about the religious training and life-style of their potential children before they get married. As I have stated previously, I believe that sharing your different perspectives on the religious upbringing of potential children, and agreeing upon a particular plan of action, ought to be a requirement of every interfaith marriage.

In general, divorce laws in the majority of states provide for a presumption of joint or shared legal custody of children. In such cases, the assumption is that both parents will share equally in all decisions relating to the child, including those that affect the child's religious upbringing. Although in general it can safely be said that joint custody tends to have great psychological benefits for the child, it can also be very confusing when it comes to religious identity and religious education.

Imagine the children who spend half their time with their mother and half with their father. One week they go to the Lutheran Sunday school with Mom and the next week are in Jewish religious school with Dad. The possibilities for complications, rivalry, jealousy, and confusion are rampant.

As Bill said in looking back over his interfaith divorce, "There wasn't really a clear agreement as there should have been in the first place. *That* must be clearly discussed and agreed upon before the marriage, or else you end up like we did with fights, arguments, heated exchanges in front of the children, and a general loss of consistency and continuity for them."

Bill's experience is common to many interfaith divorces, and it would undoubtedly be helpful for all interfaith couples to heed his warning. The lack of clarity between Bill and his ex-wife over the religious upbringing of their children led to a compromise reminiscent of a modern day twist on the wisdom of the Biblical King Solomon.

According to the legend, when two women came before him, each claiming to be the mother of a certain baby, Solomon decreed that the baby be cut in half and shared equally between them. In this story, the real mother immediately pleaded that the baby's life be spared and offered to give it to the false parent, rather than see her own child die.

In the modern day dilemma of Bill and the ex-wife, both claiming to be equally the parent, both claiming religious authority over their children, the solution was similar. As a result of their custody fight, the judge declared that their children too should be cut in half—giving the son to the father and the daughter to the mother.

In this case, however, as in so many that I know of, both parents agreed that one child was better than none, and the son is now being raised as a Jew, while the daughter is raised as a Christian. Yes, it is unpleasant to think about such things when you are in the midst of romance, love, caring, and marriage plans. But if you can, it may save both you and your children from going through an extremely painful, agonizing fight in the future over the role of religion in your children's lives.

Cooperating After the Divorce

As with marriages, the most successful divorces are those in which both parties (or rather all parties involved) force themselves to cooperate with each other all the time. It can make all the difference between your divorce going down as a recreation of the Thirty Years' War, or simply a blended family version of Ozzie and Harriet. You have the power to transcend your personal feelings about your ex-spouse and insure that you both cooperate fully for the ultimate benefit of your children. It's important that you exert that power whenever necessary, that you develop the self-discipline to overcome the pettiness that often accompanies the breakup of a relationship, and create an environment that gives a sense of security and stability to your children.

This is especially important when you have children who live in two different households. The inherent stresses on their sense of who they are and where they belong at times may seem overwhelming. Yet, you and your ex-partner *can* have a profound effect on the emotional well-being of your children, *if* you are willing to make the commitment.

The alternative to creative, supportive cooperation is to end up with more like George and Cissy's children, whose parents' interfaith divorce left them confused and religiously antagonistic to each other. "It is a little difficult for them I think, since his mother sends his sister to a fundamentalist born-again Christian school where she learns that Jews are going to hell and need to be saved through belief in Jesus, and he goes to a Jewish religious school," George said. "I never know what to say to him when he tells me that his sister is crying because she doesn't want him to go to hell and doesn't understand why he won't accept Jesus as God. I must say it puts a little strain on the family relationships."

Or, as Carol told me about her similar divorce situation, "The children are just kids, and they see the world in terms of 'right' and 'wrong.' If Daddy is right, then Mommy must be wrong, and vice versa, and with two kids each getting a different religious upbringing, it creates a real chaotic and insecure situation for them."

Don't allow yourself to fall into the same trap. For the sake of your children, agree with each other on something consistent, something that isn't subject to the capriciousness of the moment or the good feelings that happen to be warming your heart on a given day. Set limits, boundaries and direction for the role of religion in your children's lives, and you will be giving them one of the most important gifts you can in a divorce—the security to know who they are.

Taking Responsibility

Often I have heard people say that they were "pressured" into making a decision that they really did not want to make. People spend their time arguing over the *reasons* behind the decisions that they have made, rather than concentrating on the implications of the decisions themselves.

For some, it is a way of avoiding the difficult and penetrating questions that expose the very nature of their relationship. For others, it is just easier to blame an outside source for their inability to stand up for what they truly wanted, than to admit that the ultimate decision was up to them.

It is a common human characteristic to deny responsibility for our actions and decisions. It takes courage to declare, *"I* made the decision, I chose to have my life turn out this way, and whatever the results were is my responsibility as well." Instead we find a million ways of deflecting responsibility onto others.

Interfaith relationships even more than same-faith relationships need to be rooted in the solid ground of personal security and independence. Each partner needs to feel free to make the choices that will create a life of meaning, purpose, and fulfillment, while taking into account the expressed needs and dreams of the other. Life is not inherently filled with meaning. It is only filled with the ongoing *opportunity* for meaning, which each of us must create for ourselves. Even though we live in relationship to others, love them, and give as much of ourselves as we can to them, we are still ultimately faced with the reality of our personal aloneness.

For an eternity human beings have created relationships and fallen in love in a desperate attempt to transcend that inescapable chasm that separates each of us from the other.

Perhaps the story of creation as written in the Biblical book of Genesis, describing woman as having been created out of the very body of man, is an ancient primal attempt at symbolizing the fundamental need we all have to literally become one with another. The Bible even goes so far as to say directly: "and they shall become one flesh." "One flesh" is for many a consummation devoutly to be wished, for it holds the promise of merging our very being with another, losing our aloneness and the terrors of personal responsibility that accompany that separateness.

Facing our ultimate aloneness is a healthy psychological step for each of us. It can help us discover that just as we have no one to blame for our failures in life, we also deserve credit for the successes of our life.

When an interfaith relationship ends, it is all too common for each partner to fix the blame on the words, actions, or liabilities of their former partner. Instead of wasting your time and dissipating your energy in the futile avoidance of guilt and blame, acknowledge the strength within you to make the difficult choices that can ultimately bring purpose and meaning back into your life.

Use your inner resources wisely. Realize that it took courage to step into the murky waters of interfaith life in the first place. Allow yourself the luxury of a pat on the back for all that you have gone through and the strength it took to do it. Then you can acknowledge that wonderful person that is there inside and can greet tomorrow with a renewed sense of hope, faith, and trust that there really is meaning in life, because *you* will make it so.

Every upset, problem, catastrophe, separation, or divorce is like a Cracker Jack box—it always comes with a prize inside. The prize is either something important that you need to learn about yourself, an opportunity to turn your life in a new direction, or a message from your inner self that you are out of touch with what you truly want in life.

Separation and divorce are opportunities for growth and renewal. It is a time to examine those elements in your relationship that contributed to your sense of fulfillment, and those that drained you of your joy and aliveness. When did you feel most authentically you? At what times in the relationship were you most happy? Most unhappy? Most fulfilled? Most at home with yourself? Most spiritually satisfied? Most alienated from yourself?

Review the religious life-style that you created during your marriage as a way of identifying the things that gave you fulfillment, and those that left you cold and distant. Use this often painful time as a lens through which you can examine with a critical eye the life that you have been living. In this way you will discover the lessons that are there to be learned.

"When I was in the midst of the marriage, I never thought about whether I was really satisfied with the rituals and holidays we celebrated or not," Roger told me. "I was too busy just trying to keep it all together, making compromises all the time with Sherry, and arguing over a million little details of life. In retrospect, I can see that if I had been willing to express my own needs and desires clearly from the start, I would have had a better chance of getting them met.

"Her family always seemed to be lurking in the background, like a dark shadow. It wasn't that they directly interfered exactly, it was more like there was this undercurrent of always trying not to do things that would make them too hurt, upset, or disappointed with Sherry that kept creeping into all *our* decisions. One thing I learned was how important it is to take care of your own needs and live your own life. We were so worried about them all the time that we lost each other in the shuffle."

Yes, the prize is the opportunity to step back from the everyday details of running your life, to gain a new perspective on who you are and where you are going. Divorce can be like climbing the mountain and looking down upon the city below—everything looks different, fresh, and new.

Getting on with your life is the task ahead, and every ending is indeed a new beginning. Divorce, separation, loss, all are dramatic changes that place you in a large room surrounded by doors. Each door is an opportunity for new discoveries, new relationships, new directions, and new ways of thinking about yourself—but only if you gather the courage to open them.

I remember a young single parent who joined the temple. She had been recently divorced and seemed to be very angry and bitter all the time. One day I invited her into my office for a chat. I wanted to find out what it was that seemed to weigh so heavily upon her, and how I might help her to lighten the emotional burden.

When confronted with my perceptions of her pain, she confessed that she had felt relentlessly victimized by her former in-laws throughout her marriage. "It began with the wedding and continued right through the divorce," she said. "They were against the marriage from the start and were bound and determined to destroy us. Well, they sure got their wish."

I suggested that this preoccupation with blaming them for the breakup of her marriage was misdirecting her energies in destructive and unproductive ways. I told her that the very fact that she had picked herself up from the pain and loneliness of the divorce and joined a synagogue was a mark of great courage and self-worth.

It took strength of character and a knowledge of who she was and what she truly wanted out of life to seek out a religious community and make it her own. I had a lot of respect and admiration for all she had gone through, the life she was providing for her child, the values she was trying to teach, and her willingness to start life anew.

Dwelling on the past is only helpful if it gives guidance for the present. We met together several times, and eventually she told me that she had really wanted to hold on to the anger over her in-laws as a way of avoiding her own responsibility for how her life had turned out. "I think your life turns out every day," I said. "You can get up each morning and tell yourself exactly how you want the day to end, and then work to make it happen. Just look at all you have done so far. Give yourself credit for what you have done, and if you expect yourself to create miracles in your life, you will.

"Sit down with a piece of paper and make a list of all the qualities about yourself that you admire. Think of everything nice, every compliment, every casual remark from an associate or friend, every acknowledgment of your worth and character that you have ever received, and write them down.

"Use this list to build your self-confidence and feeling of self-worth. Look at it each night before you go to bed, and each morning after you wake up. Read your good qualities out loud to yourself as often as you can, until they are firmly rooted in the front of your consciousness. If you have trouble coming up with the list, make them up. Simply write down all the qualities that you would *like* to possess and recite them to yourself each day morning, noon, and night.

"Your mind doesn't know the difference between what is 'real' and what is vividly imagined. If you recite the desired qualities to yourself over and over, they will become part of your unconscious image of who you are, and you will begin to act as the person that you desire to be."

She took my advice, as I hope you will. Whenever you feel particularly down and would like to feel good about yourself, remember this true story:

A woman was once sad and depressed for days. Nothing she did seemed to help, and friends began to worry about her. One day a dozen roses arrived in the mail with a card that simply said "From someone who loves you."

She couldn't figure out who would have sent such a thoughtful gift and spent all that day and night making lists in her mind of all her relatives and friends. By the next morning she still had no idea who had sent the flowers when her sister called.

"Did you like the roses?" her sister asked.

"Oh, it was you! What a beautiful gift. Why didn't you sign the card?"

"Well, you have been so depressed for days, as if you were all alone with no one in the world to turn to. I just wanted to give you an opportunity to spend an entire day thinking of all the people in the world who love you."

Think of the roses, and of the people in the world who love you, and the world will be just a bit more beautiful once again.

EXPERIENCE
CAN BE
THE BEST TEACHER

Chapter XV

ADVICE FROM THOSE WHO HAVE BEEN THERE

"If there was one thing that I would have loved to have had prior to just jumping into my interfaith marriage headfirst, it would have been someone to talk to and ask questions of who had already experienced an interfaith relationship firsthand. That is one of the greatest gifts anyone could give to an interfaith couple."

—Walter, interfaith married ten years

Entering an interfaith marriage is in many ways an act of courage. It involves a willingness to confront individually and together the issues, pitfalls, potential stumbling blocks, and outright hostility that interfaith couples are often forced to overcome.

As we have seen from previous chapters, those who would successfully chart their course through the murky and at times treacherous waters of an interfaith marriage must develop a number of important life skills. They must be willing to discover their own true religious needs and feelings, to confront honestly the differences in background and worldview of their partner, to develop important communication skills, to overcome negative

241

stereotypes and transform them into positives, to deal sensitively with in-laws and parental disapproval, to negotiate the difficult questions regarding the raising of children and the celebration of holidays, rituals, and life-cycle events, and more.

I hope the experiences that have been shared in the pages of this book will go a long way toward making your own decisions easier. Now that we have had the opportunity to look into the lives of many interfaith couples, we will have yet one more opportunity to benefit from their combined experiences.

What follows is a collection of thoughts, "words of wisdom," and simple advice culled from the hundreds of interfaith couples and extended families with whom I have worked over the past decade. Take their advice in the spirit in which it was given—as gifts of the heart from them to you.

Each time I interviewed a couple, I would ask them the following question: "If you could speak directly to those couples about to enter into an interfaith marriage, what advice would you give them?" What follow are their answers.

Read their words with a fresh eye and an openness to their collective experiences that I hope will allow you to gain something valuable and precious as their legacy to you.

I hope you both enjoy what you are about to read and find within it advice that will relate specifically to your life and your needs.

Adam and Christy

"Live far away from your relatives for the first part of your marriage so you can be together and work out your life-style independently."

"You have to learn to talk to each other. You have to agree on things, have to have unanimity in your marriage. People who want to get married need to do serious talking with their families or agree on a united front vis-à-vis their families and others. They should each learn as much as they can about the other's religion too."

"If neither cares about their religion too much it doesn't matter, but if they do they need to make difficult decisions."

"Anything can be dealt with if you can talk about it."

"You have to learn as much as you can about your partner. You can't change them, only yourself."

Andy and Michelle

"I'd say decide for themselves what they want, and then talk to a clergy and get their help and assistance."

"If you both have strong feelings about your religion then there will be a greater likelihood for problems."

"People need to decide upon the kind of ceremony to have. If it's a problem, they need to discuss what they will be doing after the marriage—go to church, go to temple, to both? Otherwise, it's not much of a problem until you have a family. In some cases couples split up on the holidays and go to different families."

"The most important thing is to talk to each other, air your feelings, and let each do what *they* need. Communicating with each other and not keeping things inside is crucial."

"Maybe a counselor or mediator can help with communication. A third person can be helpful at times. You can't go in blind and think that it will be better later. It will probably be worse, or at least as difficult."

"There has to be compromise, and you have to be willing to not always be right."

Howard and Carol

"If both are religious then I think there will be serious problems. They should think twice before getting married at all."

Judy and Lee

"If they are religious then it makes a difference. Religion is deep-seated and to make concessions about things that you feel strongly about is a very difficult thing to do. If you do, the end result could be quite disastrous. Sincerity in any compromise is very important."

"You really need to sit down as with a business meeting to decide your future."

"It's the same in all aspects of life—to be clear about your expectations and needs within the relationship and what is really important to you."

"My best advice is 'Live your own life,' period. Yes, you want good relationships with your in-laws, but in the end it is *your* life, *your* relationship."

"Any couple in an interfaith marriage needs to establish what is important to *them* together. They need to set goals and priorities and then guide their life accordingly."

"The most important thing is for a couple to know themselves and their feelings. Don't be blinded by love so that you avoid that which is important to you. Otherwise you will make decisions and concessions that are not sincere and it will come back to haunt you in the end."

"We are best friends, and that is crucial to any healthy relationship."

Walter and Ruth

"Decide on the upbringing of the kids first, whether his or hers, but don't wait until they are born."

"One partner can't be convinced to do it the other's way. It must be a real agreement between them, a genuine compromise, otherwise the marriage won't last."

"I guess it all comes down to how important your marriage is to you. For me, it was really the most important thing in my life, and I was willing, and still am, to work as hard as is necessary to make things work out. It takes that kind of commitment to make sure that you succeed."

Heather and Eddie

"Explain all you can. Be open-minded and exposed to as much as possible about each other and each other's religion and background."

"Don't make judgments right away. Support each other, communicate, both ways are important. Don't simply be one-sided as if there is a right and a wrong."

"Don't take each other for granted."

"Go into the relationship with open minds."

"Don't close out things that you feel are important from *your* own background."

"Be supportive of each other and your families—communicate!"

"Teamwork is the key."

Jack and Diane

"It's nice to have friends to talk to and to go through it with. It's a way for us to find out about each other too, because of the questions that friends ask that we haven't even thought to talk about."

"Try to see each other and understand each other as people. Be open about things. Knowledge can't hurt, it can only help. After all, everything will come out eventually, and it is always better for it to come out sooner than later."

"Talk, talk, talk. You have to be strong together so the outside pressures don't hurt you. You have to support each other all the time. You can't use religion against someone."

Mindy and Carl

"I think it's easier to marry your own."

"It depends on how open-minded you are. It's sad to see two people in love and one with tunnel vision. Be genuinely interested in them, respect their faith, beliefs, etc."

"There are more things in life to share than religion."

"You must resolve child issues before the wedding."

Arthur and Pam

"If you find the right person and are flexible and accepting of the other's beliefs, religion per se can be worked out. You can't be dominating and demanding of the other all the time. You have to accept both religions, not necessarily believe in both, but accept them."

Deidre and Aron

"If anything is there before the marriage it will not go away. It needs to be worked out in advance. I think that people get married thinking their problems will go away, and they don't."

"I can't imagine that someone with strong religious beliefs will interdate or intermarry. It just doesn't make sense. When you are married, whatever problems exist you resent and feel trapped into. They only get worse."

Bobby and Rita

"Make decisions about your children in advance. Even if you decide not to have any, you should still decide what you would do if you did have children. You should decide upon family ties, too. How to work out family problems. Each person needs to be willing to give up some family ties for the relationship."

Maxine and Stan

"I thought after my divorce that it would be better this time to meet and marry a partner of the same faith. It just didn't work as an interfaith marriage the first time. This way it's easier, with similar family backgrounds."

"Sit down and seriously decide on religious direction. Which church or synagogue you will attend, what you choose to worship together."

"Work out decisions about which religion to choose or whether you will keep your individual religions. Come to clear understandings about how to raise the children."

"We asked each other, 'Can you wake up with me every morning and feel safe, happy, secure, and glad you made the choice?' We took our time with each other to answer all these questions, so as not to make another mistake and go through another divorce."

"Don't kid yourself. Interfaith marriages are harder and just provide one more step to overcome to make it successful."

"The most important thing in an interfaith marriage is to understand that there *will* be differences. What is important to one may not be important to the other."

"Don't hold things in. You can't sweep things under the carpet. You have to be honest, with tact of course. You must learn to express yourself in a way that will be understood by your partner."

"If you aren't happy with something that they do or are, don't think it will change or you can change it—you have to accept them as they are or not at all."

"Don't ever think that there is no room for improvement, either with yourself or the relationship. Be honest, completely above board, and be kind to each other. It is so important."

"Be caring, supportive, loving. Don't take their feelings for granted or expect they'll always understand your moods or feelings. *You can't read minds.* Talk about everything."

"Parents should let their kids work out their own problems and not take sides. Be supportive, give advice, but allow *them* to make the decision and don't punish them if they make a decision that you don't like. Don't stand in their way and say, 'I told you so.'"

Bill and Monica

"If couples aren't willing to face the real problems of their marriage, they shouldn't get married in the first place."

"It's imperative to find out the issues and discuss them all in advance. You can't put it off until some indefinite later date, because the problems are very real and simply don't go away."

"You can't necessarily go to a priest or a rabbi for advice, since they will tend to see things from their own religious perspective. I wish there was some kind of mediator service for interfaith couples that they could go to for help in dealing with these important and emotion-laden issues."

Discuss and agree upon the following issues:

"1. How to treat the holidays of the other.
"2. How to raise the children. What religion they will be and why to choose that one over the other.
"3. What happens to the religious training of the children if there is a separation or divorce. If each partner gets one child, will they be raised differently or the same?
"4. Dealing with future in-laws. How do you communicate and

what do you have to do to ensure good communication with
your in-laws and future relatives?"

"Be willing to ask, to show your ignorance. Be willing to compromise."

"You have to realize that things said in the passion of the
moment might change. We never say insulting things to each
other. It's a question of not playing dirty, ever—of having the
respect for the other person they deserve."

"You can't sink to a low level without destroying your marriage.
It's a self-respect issue as well. If you see something in the other
that you don't like and think it will go away, it probably won't. In
fact, it will probably get worse, come out more and more as the
marriage goes on. Those *must* be handled beforehand, while you
can still discuss them calmly."

"If you wait until the event itself, like the first Christmas, or the
first child comes around, you are asking for serious trouble and a
tremendous psychological blowup. Marriage and life have enough
problems anyway without deliberately causing more. If you don't
share your feelings and clear up real religious issues in advance,
you'll simply destroy the marriage."

John and Melony

"You have to decide in advance how you will raise the kids,
which parents you will visit for which holidays, which holidays
you will celebrate, and the general religious atmosphere you will
create in your home."

"Basically, you have to be honest with each other about how
you feel, particularly about religion and your beliefs. Sometimes
people say anything just to get married and don't discuss their
true feelings. You really need to be blunt about how you feel about
your religion and what is important to you."

"It would be a mistake to get married thinking that everything
will work out without clear understandings in advance. You need
to take the time to decide if you really want to spend your life with
this person, given the religion they are from and their personal
beliefs and needs."

"Be honest and open with yourselves and your partner."

"Know how important religion is to your partner."

"I think a one-religion marriage would be easier and a positive thing, so if one of you is willing to convert it would probably be a good idea."

"You must examine how important your religion is to you and then how your partner can handle it."

Paul and Steven (sixteen, fourteen)

"It's necessary for both sides to respect each other and know that they aren't going behind each other's back in raising the kids."

"Talk things out all the time. You have to know that the most important relationship is between the husband and wife. It's the responsibility of one spouse to the other that must take precedence. If there is a conflict, it always needs to be clear that the husband and wife are siding with each other against the in-laws and relatives, so each will know that the other is looking out for them all the time."

"Parents must not be afraid to tell *their* parents to knock it off, particularly when it comes to influencing the grandchildren one way or another. If necessary, you might want to try a family conference to discuss openly all the issues with your children. You should realize the pressure that is naturally a part of the lives of children of interfaith marriages."

"Parents should teach themselves about their own religions and talk to their kids about them so they will understand."

Lori (fourteen)

"If parents haven't picked a religion, they should let the kid decide. Don't pressure the child. Be free with religion so there are open options to choose from. We celebrate all the holidays in my family and the child should get a bit of everything and decide for themselves."

"Choose which religion you want, but let the kids choose too. Celebrating all the holidays is a positive experience as a child if they are more family-oriented and not really religious."

Carolyn

"Let your children do what they want to do. They wouldn't listen anyway, so what's the use in trying to change them or simply creating a rift between you?"

"If he was nice, and my daughter was happy with him, that's really all I could say. I wouldn't be overjoyed with it, but I'd be happy if they were in the end. Even if the kids were raised Catholic, I'd feel better that they had something to turn to in times of stress."

"My son, too, is grown up, and he can make his own decisions now. It's his life, and I believe in treating my grown children like adults, letting them make their own decisions in life. After all, they have to live with the consequences. I believe in only giving advice when you are asked. If either of my kids wants to know my opinion about what they are doing, I will gladly share it, but only if they ask."

"The most important thing is definitely to maintain your relationship with your children, regardless of the individual choices that they may make. It may not be your cup of tea, but that's why the store is full of teas."

Ernestine

"You really have to be supportive and go along. If your kids are that important to you, then that must be your choice. Accept what is inevitable and do the best you can. That way you *can* have an influence and stay in touch for the future."

"Either you accept the decisions that your kids make, or *you* lose out. I'm looking forward to being a grandmother now . . . I could never write my kids off. I think that is a self-defeating act. It may feel self-righteous at the time, but in the long run it has to be a mistake, like cutting your nose off to spite your face."

Well, there you have it. Clear, unadorned advice from thirty-three representative examples of couples, parents, and children, all involved in one form or another in interfaith marriages. This book has been an opportunity to stand, as it were, on the perimeter of their lives and glimpse through their discussions and revelations something of the reality of interfaith married life in America today.

We have traveled the road from discovering your own true religious feelings, through choosing a life-style, learning effective communication skills, surviving the stresses of weddings, and building relationships with in-laws of a different religious background, to the often difficult and painful decisions regarding the raising of children and the celebrations that you bring into your family's life.

We have shared together insights from those who have struggled with these life-fashioning decisions, and heard in their own words the impact that these various choices have had on their families and their marriages.

It has been said that only those who have actually experienced an interfaith marriage are in a position to give advice. Whether that is accurate or not, I believe that each of us can learn much from the life experiences of these men, women, and children who have shared themselves so generously in the pages of this book.

The world around us is in constant transition. Studies of interfaith marriage trends seem to indicate that, if anything, interfaith marriages will continue to grow as a proportion of all marriages. Those of us who care deeply about the spiritual health of our community, and are committed to the strength and vitality of individual religious communities within the great pluralistic caldron we call American society, must continue to develop creative responses to the challenges that interfaith marriages represent.

Each of us, whether involved in an interfaith marriage ourselves or simply recognizing that we are part of the matrix of American religious life, has an opportunity to truly make a difference in the quality of religious life in America. It is up to us to reach out to those couples who need our support and our love, to open the doors of our religious institutions to them and their children, to fulfill the *psalmist's dream* that "My house shall be called a house of prayer for all peoples."

It is up to each of us to help religion in America remain vibrant, relevant, alive, and adaptable to new realities and demands, so that our individual religious communities will be enriched and not engulfed.

It reminds me of the story of the Catholic boy who stayed out of school on the Jewish New Year. The next day, when his teacher asked him why he had been absent, he answered, "Because it was a Jewish holiday."

The teacher, a bit puzzled, responded, "But you're not Jewish."

"I know, but I'm in sympathy with the movement."

We all must be "in sympathy with the movement." The movement of those Christians and Jews struggling to discover their own identity and work out their destiny and the destiny of their children in the midst of an interfaith relationship. Their road is often long and treacherous, yet filled with opportunities for growth, mutual discovery, and what will inevitably be the fashioning of a new religious reality in the decades ahead.

As the face of religious America changes, we are given an opportunity to create together a community that is more accepting of individual differences, more open to change and transformation, more willing to welcome the stranger into its midst with open arms and eschew the hostility and painful rejections of the past.

Most of us share a common Biblical heritage. It is perhaps one of our greatest challenges to measure up today to the religious and social teachings of three thousand years ago. In the book of Leviticus, chapter 19, verse 34, we read one of the most eloquent and powerful, yet, if history is to be our guide, seemingly difficult commandments to fulfill in all the Bible. Were we each to follow this single commandment in our lives fully, I believe we would live in a world of peace, fulfillment, love, and joy.

I conclude this book with that Biblical dream of three thousand years ago that "the strangers who dwell among you shall be to you as the homeborn, and you shall love them as yourself."